BOILING P◼INT & COLD CASES

More Saskatchewan crime stories

Barb Pacholik
with Jana G. Pruden

U OF R PRESS

Printed and bound in Canada at Friesens.
The text of this book is printed on 100% post-consumer recycled paper with earth-friendly vegetable-based inks.

Cover and text design: Duncan Campbell, University of Regina Press.
Editor for the Press: David McLennan, University of Regina Press.
Copy editor: Anne James.
Cover photo: "Organized Crime," © Clearstockconcepts /iStockphoto.

LIBRARY AND ARCHIVES CANADA CATALOGUING IN PUBLICATION

Library and Archives Canada Cataloguing in Publication

Pacholik, Barb, 1965–, author
Boiling point & cold cases : more Saskatchewan crime stories /
Barb Pacholik, with Jana G. Pruden.

(Trade books based in scholarship ; 34)
Includes bibliographical references.
Issued in print and electronic formats.
ISBN 978-0-88977-286-1 (pbk.).—ISBN 978-0-88977-287-8 (pdf)

1. Crime—Saskatchewan. 2. Murder—Saskatchewan.
3. Cold cases (Criminal investigation)—Saskatchewan.
I. Pruden, Jana G., 1974–, author
II. Title. III. Title: Boiling point and cold cases. IV. Series: TBS ; 34

HV6809.S3P28 2013   364.1097124   C2013-904179-6   C2013-904180-X

10   9   8   7   6   5   4   3   2   1

University of Regina Press, University of Regina
Regina, Saskatchewan, Canada, S4S 0A2
TEL: (306) 585-4758 FAX: (306) 585-4699
WEB: www.uofrpress.ca

U OF R PRESS

We acknowledge the financial support of the Government of Canada through the Canada Book Fund for our publishing activities, and the Creative Industry Growth and Sustainability program which is made possible through funding provided to the Saskatchewan Arts Board by the Government of Saskatchewan through the Ministry of Parks, Culture and Sport.

 Canadian Heritage Patrimoine canadien   Government of Saskatchewan University of Regina   MIX Paper from responsible sources FSC® C016245

CONTENTS

*Denotes chapters written by Jana G. Pruden

ACKNOWLEDGEMENTS

From weighty court transcripts to a yellowed scrap of paper on which a condemned prisoner penned his plea for leniency, I revel in every archived treasure that survives to tell a tale. And when a paper trail is broken by an elusive record, I lament that lost piece of crime history doomed to be forgotten. All that is to say, each one of these stories could not have been told without the contributions, co-operation, and support of many to whom I am grateful.

I credit the resources and staff of the Saskatchewan Archives, Library and Archives Canada, Regina Public Library's Prairie History Room, and the court offices around this province.

Thank you to the fine journalists who reported many of these stories when they were still, to borrow a phrase from Knowlton Nash, "history on the run." And I give a nod to the invaluable tool of Google News Archives for making newspaper research so accessible.

My thanks also goes out to those who allowed me to tap into their memories or assisted with my research, including Rod Buckingham, Bruce Campbell, Dave Quick, Norm Marchinko, Rick Mitchell, Grant Nicurity, Jim Ralston, Brent Shannon, Maureen Wilkie, and Rob Zentner.

The support of my *Leader-Post* colleagues, past and present, was invaluable as well. In particular, I wish to thank my former co-author Jana G. Pruden for her contributions to this book, co-worker Ian Hamilton for his keen eye as a proofreader, photographer Bryan Schlosser for his time and skill with the author's photo, photographer Troy Fleece who helped me overcome some technical snags, and the newspaper's librarians who had the foresight years ago to preserve the crime and court stories.

Thank you also to fans of *Sour Milk* and *Paper Cows* for your encouragement and tips for this third book. I am indebted to Brian Mlazgar, who was the first to propose a book of Saskatchewan crime stories, to David McLennan who oversaw this third book to completion, and to the University of Regina Press (formerly the Canadian Plains Research Centre Press) for seeing the value in capturing an alternative social history of this province.

Finally, I thank my family for their patience and loving support while I disappeared to nurture this third book of crime stories and cold cases.

AUTHOR'S NOTE

In more than two decades of work as a journalist, I have often found myself with a front-row seat in court, watching cases unfold and crimes unravel. I have marveled at a con man's ingenuity (and mused about what might have been if those skills were used for good), wondered about people's motivations, smiled at foolish capers, relished dedicated sleuthing, struggled to comprehend inexplicable inhumanity, pondered how mere inches or one wrong turn could mean life or death, and admired the courage of victims. I have endeavored to capture some of those stories within these pages.

Through my research, I have journeyed back to a time when the Klan was a growing force in this province, bootlegging proved a deadly enterprise, and a killer could get away with murder in a Moose Jaw then known for its "sporting houses" of ill repute. I also went inside present-day police stings, into the minds of psychopaths, and behind the scenes of cold cases.

I have explored what people will do to or for those they profess to love, how a chance meeting can irrevocably alter lives, or why the determination of one person can make all the difference. Some themes have unfortunately proven timeless: The brutality of domestic violence, the toll of substance abuse, or the crisis of mental illness.

All of the stories in this book are recreated from true cases and capture a moment in crime. People can and do change; others prove to be beyond reform or repentance. Anything appearing between quotation marks is as it was recorded in documents or memoirs, both of which are not infallible. In some cases, those who were convicted or on whom suspicion fell maintained their innocence. I have relied on the version of events accepted by a judge or jury. Pseudonyms have been used only to comply with court-ordered publication bans and any resemblance of these names, in whole or in part, to real individuals is entirely coincidental.

Penning this third book of true Saskatchewan crime stories has reinforced one constant: Crime touches us all—whether as a victim, a community changed, or a society that bears the impact.

Barb Pacholik
2013

"Don't look for rationality in irrational acts.
We'll never know.
Probably nobody knows why this happened."

—CROWN PROSECUTOR ALISTAIR JOHNSTON
SPEAKING TO REPORTERS AT A MARCH 1996 TRIAL
FOR THE ATTEMPTED MURDER
OF AN 81-YEAR-OLD WOMAN

THE KEY

Born from frustration, desperation, anguish, and love, the letter was written by a sister to her brother. They had not spoken in at least a year, ever since Bryan McMillan vanished from the lives of his family and friends. His sister wrote to the Regina *Leader-Post*, sking the newspaper to publish her letter in the hope it might bring Bryan home.

"To my brother Bryan—wherever you are:" the letter began. It appeared in the newspaper on October 17, 1979.

"I have never missed anyone as I missed you this past year. Something has gone from my life and there is nothing to replace it and nothing can—only you.

"You can't imagine the empty feeling a family has when someone is missing: The nightmares they have about drugs, cults, and every danger there is in life. Most of all, there is a feeling of helplessness—not being able to do anything to change the situation.

"When I hold my son, I think of you and I hold him tighter, thinking maybe this will reach you, and you will come home. I want my son to know his uncle and love him …

"I see your face in crowds at high schools, pool halls, bars, everywhere. I pray I'll be walking down the street and bump into you, and am always disappointed when I don't. …"

The letter contains hints of hope—that Bryan can expect love and forgiveness from his family when he returns, that any mistakes can be mended.

"Please give us a chance," says the last line. "Tell us you are alive."

One month to the day before the appearance of the letter, the newspaper ran a short article about Bryan McMillan's disappearance, urging anyone with information to call the police. No one had seen Bryan since around 2:30 in the morning on November 8, 1978, when his friends dropped him off at a Regina house where the 18-year-old planned to spend the night. Shortly before that day, the teen had quit his job at a Kentucky Fried Chicken outlet—but his last paycheque was still waiting for him a year later. He stares out from a school photo accompanying the article: A teen with a shoulder-length mop of dark, wavy hair, barely pushed out of his blue eyes, and a slight, lopsided smile.

When the newspaper agreed to run the letter, Bryan's mother, Anne, told a reporter she wasn't sure if it would help, since the article had not yielded a single phone call.

"You never give up," Anne added, "but it seems to be a mystery."

* * *

"Come on now, Mitch. You know Bryan McMillan was murdered. Everybody knows it," Bryan's buddy told a police officer years later. "Why don't you guys do something about it?"

"Mitch" was Rick Mitchell, who joined the Regina police in July 1978 after a couple of years as a Mountie. As a street cop working in the city's north end, Rick would on occasion see Bryan and his friends hanging around. They were, for the most part, what Rick would remember decades later as "good kids."

By 1985, Mitchell was off the street and working as a resource officer at Cochrane High School when he ran into one of those "kids"—then a grown man. Brian Brown had once been a student at Cochrane. Talk turned to Bryan McMillan, who also once attended the high school. "He's been gone seven years," Brown reminded Mitchell. "What are you doing about McMillan?" he asked.

Mitchell was a high school resource officer, not a detective. But he was also missing the pace of regular policing. With time on his hands, Mitchell decided to dig up the old missing person files on Bryan. There had been a few tips over the years—rumours that suggested he wasn't a teenage runaway. But the rumours were only that, nothing concrete, no eyewitnesses.

Reading through the files, Mitchell began to make lists and a spreadsheet, setting out the tips and rumours and their sources as he tried to find some elusive pattern, anything that might provide a lead. The blue blood ran through the veins of the Mitchell family—his father, William, was a long-time cop who would become chief of the Moose Jaw force; his brother Norm was an RCMP officer. Mitchell took his lists and charts to his Mountie brother and sought the advice of aboriginal special constable Wally McNabb, working in the Fort Qu'Appelle area. Together they puzzled over the possibilities. It was McNabb who recognized the family ties that bound a number of the rumours together.

When Mitchell tracked down a woman who seemed to be the source of many of the rumours, a clearer picture began to emerge about the terrible fate of Bryan McMillan. It was the first solid lead in the cold case since 1978. And more would follow. The determined junior constable was given a desk in the robbery-homicide office, the assistance of a senior officer, and time to focus on finding Bryan's killers. Teens who had nothing to tell the police in 1978 were now young adults, some with their own children. Relationships had also changed, and the bonds that had kept them quiet for almost a decade had been loosened.

Two men were arrested in September 1985. Darrel Jerome Starr and Garth Patrick Stonechild were charged with first-degree murder. Police believed they had found Bryan's killers; but they hadn't found Bryan.

Like fitting together a jigsaw puzzle, Mitchell slowly pieced together the final moments of Bryan McMillan's life through the witnesses the cop had tenaciously tracked down all the way to Vancouver.

More like a brother than a friend, Bryan had virtually moved into Brian Brown's home in the fall of 1978. They were playing cards at the kitchen table the evening of November 8 when Darrel Starr came to the door. He was staying at the bungalow across the street, where Garth Stonechild lived with his grandmother. Starr told them he needed to buy some pot. "Jeff is going to kill me," he added, explaining that he couldn't return empty-handed to the man who had sent him to buy drugs. Brian had no interest in helping, but the other Bryan made a call. He and Darrel left together in a taxi.

When another of Bryan's friends saw the cab, it was parked outside a house about six blocks away from Brown's home. On the front lawn, Darrel had a knife in one hand, a plastic bag of pot in the other, and was still managing to hold Bryan in a headlock.

When Bryan returned to Brown's house, he was nursing what he suspected were three broken ribs. He also had a nasty gash over his left eye and a very sore head. "Darrel Starr did this to me," he said, rushing into the house.

Brown and McMillan left a couple of hours later when a friend, who had a job delivering pizzas, called because he had run out of gas. The pair went to bail him out. After making the gas delivery, they separated, with plans to meet up at a party. But when Bryan and his other friends came by, there was no one there. It was around 2:30 a.m. when they dropped Bryan off at the back of Brown's house.

Anyone who had seen him after that never told the story until Mitchell came knocking seven years later.

Garth Stonechild's girlfriend dropped by his house on her way to school that morning. Garth, wrapped up in a blue down-filled jacket, was asleep on his bed in a basement bedroom. Darrel also lay there asleep. On the floor next to the bed was a young man, face down and naked. She recognized him as Bryan McMillan, who sometimes came over to play cards. It reminded her of how Garth used to steal her clothes when he didn't want her to leave.

A 10-year-old boy was leaning over Bryan. "Come on

McMillan, get up," said the boy. "Why did you be so mouthy last night?" The girl saw the bruises on Bryan's back and shook awake 16-year-old Garth, telling him that Bryan looked dead.

She told the child to pull a blanket over Bryan, then stepped out of the bedroom with her boyfriend. "He's dead," she told him. "You'd be cold too if you slept on the floor all night," Stonechild replied. A few minutes later, Darrel Starr joined them, saying, "Bryan's dead." The two young men spoke of getting rid of the body before Stonechild's grandma got home that night. Garth also said something about how he had peed in Bryan's mouth.

Darrel Starr turned to a cousin for a car. He said they had beaten up a guy with a hockey stick and drowned him. Now they needed to borrow a car to use to hide the body. "We didn't mean to do it," Starr told another teenage girl, who had also seen Bryan lying on the floor when she got to the house sometime around 3 or 4:00 a.m.

They kept Bryan's body in a closet beneath the stairs throughout the day. As darkness fell, Garth and Darrel took Bryan's corpse out and pulled on his clothes. Garth removed the blue jacket that he'd worn most of the day and returned it to its rightful owner, McMillan. They rolled him in blankets and a carpet. Lifting the bundle onto their shoulders with the help of two others, they carried it outside. They put Bryan's body in the trunk of a light blue Chevy and drove away. An hour or so later, Darrel and Garth returned to the house.

No one spoke any more about Bryan.

* * *

A preliminary hearing was held almost seven years to the day after Bryan vanished. The police and prosecution still couldn't produce a body, but they had enough circumstantial evidence to prove he had been killed. Stonechild and Starr were committed to stand trial for murder.

Mere days before they were to choose a jury, the defence had a proposal for the prosecution.

Stonechild left the Regina Correctional Centre—at least temporarily. Rick Mitchell sat in the back seat with him during the car ride. He had no idea where they were going; his prisoner did. Without any hesitation, Stonechild quietly gave directions for their destination as the police car left behind the jail on Regina's eastern outskirts on May 21, 1986, and headed towards the city. He said little, but for the odd, "turn here."

On Stonechild's direction, Staff Sergeant Norm Marchinko steered north from the Trans-Canada Highway, past the television tower on the city's outskirts, then east along a grid road. "Stop right here," Stonechild said, as the car neared a bluff of willow trees some eight miles northeast of Regina.

"We dropped him in the bush and drove away."

Mitchell waited in the vehicle with his prisoner while Marchinko and the other officers who were part of the entourage walked about 20 feet into the bluff. In an open area circled by willows, they spotted the bundle callously discarded eight years earlier. It was covered by the debris of dirt, leaves, and twigs that had fallen or blown in over the course of nearly a decade but was otherwise in the open.

The remnants of a young man's life were there—mostly bones, but also a pair of brown leather boots, a belt, and pants.

Marchinko reached into the pocket of the pants and pulled out a set of keys.

"Yeah," he told Mitchell upon returning to the car, "he's there."

* * *

The deal was sealed in a Regina courtroom. Stonechild and Starr pleaded guilty to the lesser offence of manslaughter. Through their lawyers, they denied using a hockey stick on Bryan or drowning him, but Stonechild admitted that he had started a fight and pushed Bryan down the stairs, and that Starr had joined in by kicking and hitting the teen. People who knew the men sent letters to the court saying that such violence was uncharacteristic of them. One First Nations chief wrote to extend his sympathies to the McMillans and added that Starr had been tormented by what had occurred.

Over the years, usually when he had been drinking or using marijuana, Starr would let something slip out about that day back in November 1978. Only that past spring before his arrest, when his cousin's children were making gurgling noises in the bathtub, Starr had remarked how Bryan had once made the same sounds. Now, a year later, in May of 1986, Starr rose to his feet in the courtroom to speak. "It's caused me great pain ...," he said before breaking down. "It has caused—caused—caused me great pain to live with what I've done, but I learned to respect ..." He was unable to finish. A grown man of 27, he cried like a child.

Stonechild was 24 years old when he admitted he had been the instigator in Bryan's death. Back then, he had been 16, almost the same age as the man he killed. "I'm sorry for what I've done," he told the judge. "But at the time I was young. I didn't realize what I was doing. And now I realize there's a better way of life that I can look forward to hopefully in the future."

Justice Ted Malone had the final word: "Whatever feelings of remorse you both may have pale in significance when I consider the agony the family of the deceased must have suffered."

After Bryan was found and before his killers were each sentenced to five years in prison, Mitchell and Marchinko took the keys removed from the tattered, weathered pants in the tree bluff. They went to the Regina house where the McMillans had raised Bryan and his two brothers and the sister who had written her heartfelt letter so many years before, trying to tell her brother how one day, with maturity, he would come to appreciate that his parents were also his best friends. Bryan's father, John, passed away in 1981; his mother, Anne, followed a year later. They died never knowing why their youngest son had never come home.

Eight years later, Bryan's key still opened the door.

BITTER WIND

"**T**here's been an accident," John Harms said, standing in the doorway of Anne's little shack on a cold November afternoon. "Johnny hurt himself. He had a fainting fit. Can you come and see what you can do?"

Anne didn't want to go.

She was alone in the cabin with her young son, and Ira, the trapper she lived with, would be out on the trapline for a few more days at least. There was no one else anywhere nearby in the northern Saskatchewan wilderness.

Anne Lindgren didn't trust John Harms. He had always been nice enough to her when he was sober, but he was different when he was drinking, and she could smell the alcohol on him now.

She had been afraid of him since that day down by the water, when John followed her as she was filling her pails, then came towards her with his pants open, pushing her down and trying to touch her body. He didn't stop until Johnny Anthony saw them from the lake and paddled in to shore to help her.

Johnny had grabbed John by the arm and pulled the old man away from her.

"Behave yourself and be a gentleman," Johnny had told him with disgust. When John was gone, Johnny came back to help Anne carry her full water pails up to the cabin.

John and Johnny became trapping partners in the summer

of 1935, and had been living together at the cabin across the lake from Anne for about six months.

To Anne, the men were almost like father and son. The younger Johnny was always able to keep John in line, even though John was so much bigger, and was so quarrelsome and quick to anger when he drank the homebrew he made from malt sugar, yeast cakes, potatoes, and rice.

But Johnny wasn't around to help Anne now.

And John was at her door, stinking of homebrew and asking her to come with him into the freezing wind.

"I don't think I can," she said. "It's too late."

"Yes," he told her. "You are going to come."

John's eyes told her she could not say no.

Anne bundled her baby into a heavy parka, then walked with John to his dogsled.

The old dogs started off, pulling the sleigh slowly along the two-mile stretch to John's cabin. As they travelled, John sang for a while, not seeming as drunk as he had before.

At one point, he looked at the child in Anne's arms, then took the boy's head in his hands, squeezing the boy's skull between his strong fingers until Anne cried for him to stop.

John told her he would like a photograph of her and her son.

"I would give a million dollars for a snapshot," he said. "One snapshot."

When they finally pulled up to the cabin, John told Anne to go inside.

"This is going to be a shock to you," he warned as she approached the door.

With no fire lit, the cabin was dark and freezing. Anne could barely see Johnny lying on the floor. She called his name, but he didn't answer.

"What's wrong?" she asked John, who had walked into the cabin behind her.

"That's what you are going to find out," he said.

John struck a match, and as it flared, Anne saw the truth in the flickering yellow light. There was blood running from a bullet wound in Johnny's neck, pooling in a cold, deep puddle underneath him on the cabin floor.

Anne turned and ran. With her son clutched to her chest, she ran as fast as she could across the frozen lake, the wind biting into her face as she scrambled on the ice and rocks.

A gun went off behind her.

She heard the report of the shot, the whine of the bullet as it flew through the frozen willows, whizzing close by her legs and hitting the ice nearby.

She could hear John getting back in his sleigh, directing the dogs back towards Anne's cabin. She thought for a moment about hiding in the bush, but she knew it was too cold for her and the baby to survive outside for long, so she just kept running into the wind, across the frozen lake towards home.

John beat her there, but was slumped unconscious on his sled when Anne walked quietly up from the shore.

She slipped past John and the dogs and went inside, immediately barricading the front door and windows of her shack with whatever she could find.

Her only protection was two butcher knives and a small rifle with six shells. She loaded the gun and waited for John to wake up.

* * *

John Harms had been born in Germany, but moved to the United States as a young man and spent years bouncing around from place to place, job to job. He had been a rancher in Ohio, a farmer in Idaho. He spent two years as a police officer, then put in 10 years underground in the mines of Nevada. He operated a saloon for a while, before finally heading north to the unexplored Canadian wilderness.

John was well known in the north country, and many people had been guests at his cabin, which was known as a place where you would find a hearty welcome and could stay free of charge. Several priests and a bishop were among those who had enjoyed John's hospitality.

John became trapping partners with Johnny Anthony in the summer of 1935, the two men sharing their traplines and living together in the small cabin on the desolate north shore of Lake Athabasca, about 75 miles north of Goldfields.

John was 65, Johnny 31. For the most part they got along fine as roommates and business partners, except when John started drinking.

A few weeks earlier, John had made a batch of home-brew to celebrate a moose they shot, and he'd been drinking steadily every since.

On the afternoon of November 23, John had gone into a rage, convinced that his partner was holding out a mink pelt on him.

"You goddammned son of a bitch," John yelled at him.

"Shut up," Johnny had said. "I'll talk to you when you are sober."

* * *

John Harms stayed outside Anne's cabin for four days. Sometimes he would hammer at the door, swearing and hollering and rattling the windows while she sat inside with her son, clutching the gun, loaded and ready to fire. Other times, he was quiet.

John built a fire, and he spent hours sitting silently on caribou hides he had set out near the blaze, roasting moose meat, and thawing out beer. A few times he left for an hour or two, just enough time for Anne to slip out of the cabin and get water and firewood, then hurry back inside to barricade the cabin once again and await his return. On the third day, John yelled that he would freeze to death if Anne didn't let him inside, but still she would not open the door.

On the fourth day, John called out that he was going to his other cabin on Singed Dog Island and that the police could come get him there. Then he left on his dog sleigh.

When Ira Allen finally came home to his shack later that day, Anne told him what had happened, and the trapper immediately headed to Goldfields to get a message to the RCMP.

* * *

Sergeant Fitzpatrick "Pat" Vernon got word of the murder on December 3, in a telegram from Stanley Wylie, a Hudson's Bay Company trader who had met Ira in Goldfields.

The Mountie set out that same night with Irwin Villobrough, a native interpreter, to find John Harms and arrest him for murder.

The men camped two nights, slowed by a snowstorm that brought plunging temperatures and a bitter wind. When they got in sight of John Harms' cabin at Singed Dog Island, they decided to wait until dawn to approach, just in case the old man might be tempted to shoot it out.

Pilot Lewis Leigh was able to land his craft in the snow nearby and joined the other men to help with the arrest.

But as the three men approached at dawn with guns drawn, they found John Harms waiting and ready to surrender. He waved a white piece of cloth to show his intentions.

"I'm glad you came," he told Sergeant Vernon.

"What seems to be the trouble, John?" the officer asked.

"I will tell about it later."

The men then travelled back to John Harms' other cabin, where they found Johnny dead on the floor, frozen solidly into his own blood. There were 17 empty beer bottles on a shelf in the kitchen, and two 10-gallon barrels in an outside shed: one full of meat, the other full of beer mash. The mink pelt that sparked the disagreement was hanging frozen behind the stove. Sergeant Vernon seized it as evidence for the trial.

* * *

John Harms was convicted of murder in February 1936, and sentenced to be executed that spring. Defence lawyer John Diefenbaker appealed the conviction and verdict on the grounds of self-defence, drunkenness, and provocation, and won his client a new trial.

Testifying in his own defence, Harms said he didn't know exactly what he did to his partner and only remembered waking up in bed, wet, and with his gun missing.

An expert on intoxication testified that revolver shooting required a "high degree of coordination," which would be impacted by being drunk. Diefenbaker also raised the spectre that Johnny Anthony had threatened his roommate, and had been attempting to strangle him when he fired the fatal shot.

A new jury convicted Johns Harms of manslaughter in June 1936, and he was sentenced to 15 years in the penitentiary.

The case made headlines around North America, with papers running accounts of Anne Lindgren's four-day ordeal inside the cabin and the RCMP officer's harrowing journey to find the killer.

It seemed a truly Canadian tale.

The *Palm Beach Post* declared that a "two day dash by dog team over 90 miles of rough ice and deep snow of the lonely north country" added "another epic chapter to the history of the famed Canadian mounted police." The *Spokane Daily Chronicle* said the trapper of Singed Dog Island showed "glamour still exists north of 55," and proved that "the Mounties always get their man."

WHEELS OF JUSTICE

Her curves were beautiful—the lines smooth, graceful, memorable. She was sleek, with a hint of something contemporary and unpredictable in the V-shaped chrome grille, the moon hubcaps, and the bullet headlights set into the fenders.

The attractive design and restyled engine of the 1938 Chrysler had caught the eye of businessman-farmer John Kaeser. He bought the grey coupe new that spring. It was admittedly a bit of flashy luxury, but Kaeser, known as a leader in mechanized farming, was what his neighbours would describe as "comfortable."

Business brought the well-dressed gentleman and his coupe to Regina from his Moosomin home. Kaeser always stayed at the LaSalle Hotel, where the bellhops knew him to be a good tipper. His business affairs concluded after three days, Kaeser set out that morning in his Chrysler—only to return within hours. He was barely outside Regina when he heard the sickening sound of steel on steel and reached vainly for the pistol-grip handbrake. But it was too late. The truck had side-swiped Kaeser's car, maiming the driver's side fenders and door.

The automobile went to the garage, its owner back to the LaSalle.

The car was almost perfect—of course, it would never be exactly so—when the garageman delivered it to Kaeser at the hotel four days later, on November 9, 1938. With his two bags loaded in the trunk, Kaeser topped off the gas tank, paid his bill at the garage, then headed out on the highway again.

Despite the new winter ground grips on the rear, the coupe still ended up stuck in the snow during a stop near Balgonie to drop off groceries for a friend. Kaeser, anxious to get home before the roads got worse, declined an offer to come inside and instead retrieved his shovel from the trunk and put it to work. Fifteen minutes later, he waved goodbye and drove off.

* * *

The driver was headed to a Ford convention in Regina and only too happy to offer a lift to the young hitchhiker he met just outside Estevan. They exchanged his 1938 Ford for his older Ford sedan in Weyburn, then carried on to the city, chatting about how the young man had been working on his uncle's farm near Arcola but was now looking for work in the city.

From Regina, the young man caught a lift in a truck east down the highway, getting as far as McLean.

Avis Smith, the town's postmistress, answered a knock at the door to find a stranger in search of a bed for the night. Smith's mother, Henrietta, felt sorry for the quiet, mannerly young man and agreed to put him up for the night. He left the next morning, around nine o'clock on November 9, leaving a note promising to send 75¢ to pay for his room since he had no money. He signed his name H. McFarlane, gave a Winnipeg address, then headed off for the highway to try to hitch another ride.

* * *

Joseph Winter was hauling straw to the Trout farm near Sintaluta when he spotted the light grey Chrysler. The farmhand brought his bobsleigh and team of horses to a stop to let the automobile go past. A young man with dark, slicked-back brown hair occupied the driver's seat. "He had very large ears," Winter would later remark.

It was, in the words of Eva Trout, "a lovely sun-shiny day" when she saw the two-door car around 11:00 a.m. Expecting company, she was sweeping the back steps and watched the grey coupe turn off the highway and head south across the railway tracks.

But Eva didn't recognize the car that pulled into the lane and stopped beside a small bluff of willow trees. A few minutes passed before she saw any movement, then a man exited from the driver's door, walked to the front, then around to the passenger door, where he stooped over as if working at something. After a bit, he returned to the driver's side, then back to the right. Once, he walked up about 10 feet in front of the vehicle. He must be shovelling himself out of the snow, Eva thought. After 15 minutes, the car turned around in the field and drove off east down the highway.

James Woodland was standing on a hill just outside Brandon when the Chrysler pulled to a stop. The 26-year-old had been adrift the last five years, usually riding the freight trains, illegally of course, but occasionally begging rides from strangers. Woodland thanked the driver as he slid into the passenger seat and explained that he was headed to Portage la Prairie in search of work. The driver suggested Winnipeg, where he was going, might present more opportunities, and Woodland agreed.

They were a ways down the road when Woodland noticed the stains on the passenger door, steering wheel, and dashboard.

The driver, noticing his passenger gazing at those damned stains, told Woodland how he had been duck hunting south of Brandon. Not quite dead when he got it in the car, one of the bagged birds had started wildly flapping around, getting blood all over the car, he said.

The driver picked up speed, hitting 90 miles per hour. He told Woodland he was going to be late for work. They made a brief pit stop at a station in McGregor for sandwiches and milk—the driver's treat since Woodland had no money. He also paid when they ran out of gas a few miles further along, and for a tow when they inevitably hit the ditch at those speeds. Still, they made good time. It was shortly after six o'clock that evening when Woodland climbed out of the car in Winnipeg.

About an hour later, the driver showed up at Margaret Kroeker's rooming house. The man—Margaret hadn't caught his name or where he was from—carried two club bags, one black and the other brown, with monogramed gold lettering: "JAK."

Sixteen-year-old Bert Taylor noticed the grey car outside his Furby Street house the next day. At Bert's urging, his mother called the police to report the coupe with the Saskatchewan licence plate. But the police told her no such car had been reported stolen, so no one showed up.

Another call on Friday brought a couple of police officers, who checked it out, then left. Taylor's mom mentioned the red stains her son had noticed, but the officers said that wasn't so unusual during duck-hunting season.

And so the coupe remained until that night, when two men got in and drove off.

Arnold Graham had asked if he and his friend could borrow the car. Although he didn't have a licence, his buddy Jack did. The pair tooled around all over the city, out to the airport, and over to the suburbs on the west side. At some point, Jack noticed the steering seemed a bit wonky. He stopped and asked Arnold to check the tires, which he did. As Arnold slid back into the passenger seat, the gabardine coat he'd been sitting on shifted, revealing a large stain on the seat. At Arnold's urging, Jack looked too. Arnold even turned on the dome light, and discovered that wasn't the only stain. There were splashes of what looked like blood on the passenger door and the running boards. Jack showed him a crescent wrench, which also seemed to have stains on it. Arnold threw it out the window.

Suddenly feeling ill and with the joy gone from the ride, Arnold opted to take a streetcar home, leaving Jack with the car. Jack promptly abandoned it on a residential street.

When Arnold got back to the rooming house, he wanted to know about those stains. It was starting to make sense why Harry Heipel, Jack's brother, had been reluctant to hand over the keys to that car.

"I had been hitchhiking and this man picked me up," Harry said in response to Arnold's questions. "I hit this man on the head with the wrench, and dragged his body to the side of the road, and drove the car away."

When he got back to the room, Jack didn't bother with an explanation. He knew better than to ask his brother for one. But Jack did ask that Harry remove the two bags he had left in Jack's room as well as a wallet, embossed with J. A. Kaeser.

Mrs. R. Aldiss called police on Saturday about the suspicious-looking car parked outside her house. Despite the stormy weather, the car's windows were rolled halfway down and the keys had been left inside. This time, the police took notice—and learned its owner, John Kaeser, had been expected home a few days earlier by his wife.

Eva Trout caught only part of the police report on the radio that morning—something about a blood-stained car and a search for a missing man. She made a point of listening for the afternoon report. When she heard about the discovery of the 1938 grey Chrysler coupe, she thought back to the vehicle she had seen five days earlier. "Surely that must be the car," Eva thought.

Determined to prove her theory, the grey-haired farm woman pulled on her boots and coat and waded through the snow to the tree bluff. She stopped and looked back at the weathered farmhouse, making sure she was in the right spot. Wading into the thigh-deep snow in the trees, she came upon a small clump of willows that appeared to be pressed down by some weight. She steeled her nerves and stepped closer. Her eyes fell first on a blanket, then a man's boot—and finally an ankle and pant cuff.

Having seen enough, Eva hurried home. The police came later that night. In the darkness broken only by the lights on the police car, Eva showed them the spot, pointing out the ankle and the boot.

John Kaeser's bullet-riddled body was laid out at the undertaker's in Sintaluta when Dr. Frances McGill arrived the next day to conduct the post-mortem. It took the pathologist two days to complete her examination because the 65-year-old farmer was so terribly frozen. She found four bullets in the corpse—two in his head and two in his back. They had also wounded his groin and arm.

His suit coat pocket still carried his receipt from the Saskatchewan Motor Company for the $49.98 in repairs on the coupe, and a notice for a meeting of Moosomin Masonic Lodge, of which he was a long-time member. A search of the dead man's pockets also turned up a 65-cent receipt for a phone call to Moosomin, a blank sheet of paper from the LaSalle, a bank book for his savings account, $9.82 in cash, a gold pocket watch monogramed with JAK—and Kaeser's lucky rabbit's foot.

Police had the car and Kaeser; now the hunt turned to his killer.

Winnipeg police officers showed up at Jack's rooming house a day after news of the car hit the Monday papers and tips started to pour in about sightings of the grey coupe. A search of Jack's room turned up four ties and some toothpaste, taken from Kaeser's bags and left by Harry. But the wanted man, who had left Kaeser's two club bags in a locker at Union Station, was nowhere to be found.

Police had a pretty good idea where he might be headed.

The parents of Harry and Jack had divorced when the boys were nine and eight, respectively. Neither their father, a train conductor, nor their mother, who moved south to Illinois, was too eager to raise their sons, who were instead shuffled between relatives. As a teen, Harry did join his mother in the States, where he racked up convictions for larceny and forgery, the last offence landing him in the Illinois State Penitentiary for 15 months. In March 1938, he had been deported to Canada.

As Kaeser's wife, adult daughter, and scores of townsfolk gathered for his funeral in Moosomin, an international hunt was on for Harry.

Ten days after Kaeser and his repaired coupe had headed down the highway for home, and Harry had stood on that same roadway looking for a ride, a farmer spotted Harry walking on a road near Rockford, Illinois. He recognized the young man, who had been friendly with his daughter when he lived in Illinois two years earlier. She had broken off the relationship shortly before he went to prison.

Now Harry was working on a farm in the area. That night, Harry joined his employers for an outing. As they watched the leading men get their gals in *Talent Scout* and *Roaring Timber* at the picture show in Rockford, Illinois, Sheriff Delos Blanchard was setting out a plan to get his man. When the car carrying Harry and the couple pulled into a garage, Blanchard and the officers moved in to arrest the fugitive.

Harry told the sheriff he didn't know anything about a murder, having found Kaeser's car while hitchhiking.

There was no trouble finding a ride to Regina this time. The 24-year-old wanted man with the pale, boyish face was whisked off the 7:00 a.m. train in darkness on November 24, 1938.

Kaeser's beloved grey coupe also came back to Regina, where it and the man seen behind the wheel were identified by those who had encountered the two.

Never seen again was a .38-calibre revolver that had disappeared from an Arcola-area farm home where Harry sometimes visited. Most people who had seen the pistol remembered the shine from the nickel plating and the unique bone handle grip. And they remembered Harry trying to sell such a gun to friends in Estevan.

The bullets fired from the revolver also had a memory—and those pulled from Kaeser's body matched perfectly with the ones pulled from the barn that Harry used for target practice. Harry had come to Saskatchewan and found work near Arcola on the farm of Robert McFarlane, a distant relative but one whose surname he didn't mind borrowing when he signed the promissory note in McLean or crossed the border to the United States while on the run.

It was a circumstantial case, to be sure—following the path of a hitchhiker and a car—but it took the jury no more than nine hours to find Harry guilty.

Harry gripped the railing in front of the prisoner's dock as Justice Anderson passed sentence, then slumped to his chair. Tears ran down the young man's cheeks as the judge thanked the six-man jury. As Harry was escorted away, Arnold Graham and Jack's brother, key witnesses against him, stepped into a side room where their tears gave way.

Harry's lawyer made a plea for clemency for a boy who veered off the right path in life through no fault of his own. He grew up without the "virtuous care" of a mother or the "wise guidance of a kindly, judicious father."

Even five of the six jurors signed a letter to the justice minister asking for clemency. Juror Fred Dixon wrote: "Knowing how sympathetic we were to the accused and how reluctant—at least five of the jurors were—for the extreme penalty of the law to be imposed, I am convinced that if the judge had pointed out it was within our power to bring in a recommendation for mercy, it would have been done most strongly."

A letter also came from Ethel Montgomery of Winnipeg. A friend of hers roomed in the house where the two boys were placed by their father, who paid a large fee for their care. But she said they were "shamefully abused" by those who were paid to care for them. "Brutally beaten," they were sent to sell newspapers on the street and the money taken from them, she wrote, adding that Harry used to plead for the brute to spare his brother.

"In all probability, this may have laid the seed which caused the boy to do wrong," she added.

Two ministers who had been visiting Harry in prison also wrote—prompting a letter of his own from a Moosomin farmer. "The people of this district who knew Kaeser as a likeable, upright man, look upon his murder as probably one of the most brutal in the annals of Canadian crime," he said.

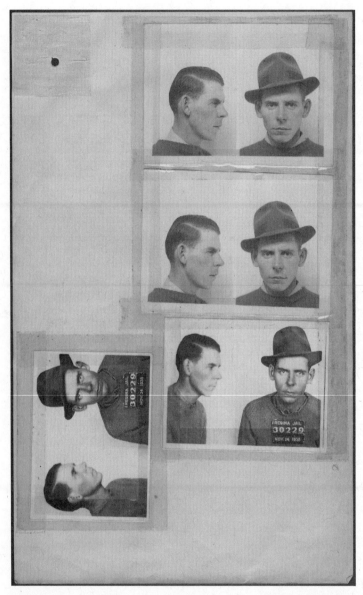

Harry Heipel, ca 1939. Copyright Government of Canada. Reproduced with permission of the Minister of Public Works and Government Services Canada (2011). Source: Library and Archives Canada/Department of Justice fonds/RG 13-B-1. File cc 496, Item 71725.

Even reluctant Crown witness Arnold Graham wrote, seeking clemency for his friend. "He has never had a break in life, but he needs one now."

It was dated April 19, 1939.

Six days later, a telegram was sent from Ottawa to the sheriff in Regina: "I hereby confirm that the law will take its course in the case of Harry Heipel."

And so it did the next day at the Regina jail.

Despite a chill wind, about three hundred people jammed the street outside the funeral home later that afternoon. They caught a glimpse of Harry's brother, Jack, and their father. And they watched as the funeral cortège moved to the cemetery, taking Harry on his last ride.

A ROSE BY ANY OTHER NAME

S ure, it was only a patch of mud and tufts of grass for now, but Paul Mushansky liked to stand there and think about what it would become. He walked past the corner daily, looking longingly for the big trucks and other heavy equipment. Paul wanted to be there to witness first-hand his bare parcel of land getting carved and moulded—transformed from vacant lot to home. He'd always wanted a house on a corner lot. And this is where it would be, on the southeast corner of St. John Street and Fourth Avenue North.

As a cleaner for the City of Regina, Paul was not a wealthy man. But when he saw the advertisements in the *Leader-Post* in the winter of 1958, he felt certain the dream of him and his wife owning their own home was in reach. For only a small down payment, Adams Construction Company would build a house, lot included. And better yet for Paul, the company was willing to take a vehicle in lieu of a down payment. Paul owned a 1954 Chevy.

After several phone calls, Paul went to the offices of Adams Construction and met personally with owner William Adams. They discussed location, cost, and terms. On February 2, 1959, Paul gave his car to Adams as a $1,500 down payment on a two-bedroom bungalow. To save on costs, Paul and his wife planned to move into the basement while the house was under construction. Paul asked about seeing some of the other houses the company had on the go. But Adams didn't like to show someone else's house to another customer.

"You'll see the house when it's built," he promised. "You won't go wrong." Adams said he would get the paperwork ready and Paul could come by in a couple of weeks and sign it. Paul did come by a few times, but it never seemed to be the right time. Adams was always away from his office. One day Paul caught up to the contractor just as he was leaving. "I'm so busy," Adams said, suggesting Paul return the next day. Another three or four weeks passed before they connected again. The paperwork still wasn't done, but Adams told Paul the workers should start to dig the basement in about a week, and the house would be finished come June.

Excitement was building for the Mushanskys. Because he didn't have a car, Paul walked by the vacant lot day after day. But there was never any activity. Nothing.

He went back to Adams' office that April, but once again the contractor wasn't there. It was a Saturday, after all, thought Paul. He returned on Monday—only to find the office as vacant as his corner lot. Paul had his receipt for the car signed by H. W. Adams, and little else. He went to City Hall to check on his lot. That's when he found out it wasn't his lot at all. It belonged to another man, a merchant who had bought the lot about six years ago.

Paul was not the only one looking for Adams.

Frank and Emma Hoffman had also hired Adams Construction. They were advised by a real estate agent that Adams could build more cheaply than anyone else in the city. The elderly couple wanted an eight-suite apartment block. Adams said he could do it for $40,000, so they put down a $2,000 deposit on December 5, 1958. The Hoffmans were actually $44 short in their account when Adams went to cash the cheque, so Adams reached into his own pocket to deposit the shortfall in order to cash the cheque.

The Hoffmans kept pressing for blueprints and a contract—but Adams was always out of town or too busy. He finally came over one evening and showed them some plans, but they weren't really what the couple wanted. Adams said he could have the right plans in a week or two, but he would need more money. In January, the Hoffmans reached into what was left of their savings and put down another $2,000. Adams still didn't have the blueprints, but he did provide a written statement promising construction on their apartment at Central Street and 18th Avenue would start by May 30, or their money would be refunded.

It wasn't.

By the time William Harold Adams was located that July—arrested in Burnaby, British Columbia, for contributing to the delinquency of a juvenile—the Adams Construction Company was bankrupt. Close to 90 prospective homeowners and companies were out some $120,000, nearly $1million in today's dollars.

Gordon Dean Rose—alias Adams—would never face trial for that amount. The police settled on eight of its strongest cases and charged him with those, frauds totalling $15,756.

Looking every inch the businessman he claimed to be, a well-groomed Rose, handsomely dressed in a grey suit, appeared in court in March 1960 for the first of his trials. Postal clerk Kenneth Moldovan had stroked Adams a $1,700 cheque and was also supposed to turn over his 1956 Dodge Regent, valued at $1,600, on deposit for his $14,000 house. Adams never did get the car.

"In checking on some of the things, I found they weren't all up to what was supposed to be," Moldovan testified. Adams didn't actually own the lot where he was supposed to build Moldovan's house.

Midway into his third trial—the previous two having ended in convictions—Rose a.k.a. Adams knew there was no digging himself out of this hole.

"I have been going over this thing thoroughly, and I think, Your Worship, that it is just a waste of time for me to argue these things," Rose told the court. He pleaded guilty to the remaining charges.

The prosecution urged the judge to take a dim view of Rose's schemes. "The police department here has information that the accused has operated in several points in Canada, very similar types of operation although this is the first time he has ever been prosecuted," city prosecutor John Malone said.

Adams had opened up shop in Regina in the fall of 1958, renting out office space and hanging out a shingle as a building contractor. His newspaper ads promised a house and a lot by the spring of 1959— and at a $3,000 savings.

But Rose suggested he too had been a victim. "As it stands now, it is about $30,000 of mine that has disappeared from the business somewhere."

"Where?" asked the judge.

"I don't know," replied

Gordon Dean Rose, 1960. Reproduced with permission from the Regina *Leader-Post.*

Rose, explaining how he left in April for a business trip to Vancouver and returned to find $69,000 equity in his business gone. "I have made many mistakes," he concluded.

"This is more than a mistake," Magistrate E. L. Elliott fired back. "You have taken the bread out of the mouths of old people and working people. It is about as low a deal as has ever been before me. I think it is the lowest. It reaches the all-time low."

Such a low, thought Elliott, deserved a high. Each of Rose's crimes carried a 10-year maximum term in prison.

"I can't imagine a man more devoid of conscience than you appear to be. You are not safe to be at large for the protection of other people. That is what I think about you and this silly story that you are telling now isn't going down at all," Elliott added.

"I don't think you care as long as you save your own precious skin. My idea is the place for you is on the inside looking out." Elliott delayed sentencing to Friday the 13th in May 1960 before making up his mind. Then he sentenced 29-year-old Rose to a total of 10 years in prison.

"Unless you change, you are a menace to the public to be at large, at all," Elliott said.

Rose wasn't about to let Elliott have the last word. He filed an appeal. In a letter to the appeal court, Elliott was as unrepentant as Rose.

"I feel that the probabilities are that if and when this man is released, he will start up a similar fraud in some other place, possibly in some other way," Elliott wrote in June 1960. "I know the sentence is severe, but I think his is a case of where it should be left to the parole board to decide when they are satisfied that Adams has had a change of heart, and he is fit to be returned to society.

"I suspect this man is a psychopath and improvement unlikely for a very long time," Elliott added.

Five months later, the Saskatchewan Court of Appeal cut Rose's 10-year prison term in half.

More than a decade later, in 1973, a man calling himself Gordon Dean Rose was sentenced in an Edmonton courtroom for fraud. The 42-year-old was serving time in a British Columbia prison when he stumbled upon a new way to make some easy money in the prison hobby shop. While out on passes from prison, where he was serving time for forgery, he spent counterfeit $50 bills that he claimed to have fashioned while in the big house.

Fast-forward to 1985 when, in a Winnipeg courtroom, a Gordon Dean Rose pleaded guilty to nine counts of fraud, drawing a five-year prison sentence. "You are, without a doubt, one of the most unsuccessful con men I've ever encountered," the judge told the convict in his 50s. Rose, known by a variety of names, had been contracted to do repair and renovation work to homes in Manitoba and Saskatchewan, but took the money and ran. Rose also collected down payments from several Saskatoon residents for an apartment he didn't own.

Back in 1960, a police officer had marvelled at the skill of Adams/Rose. "He was a super salesman," he told a *Leader-Post* reporter. "And maybe something of a magician."

INSIDE MAN

The vehicles were parked about a half mile out of town. They were big cars, two Cadillacs, the roomy sort made for carrying seven passengers—or 35 cases, 50 if the contents of those cases were transferred to sacks. There was also a Buick Roadster. It could only handle about 21 cases loose.

The six men divided between the cars were on edge as they hid in the darkness. When they had seen the headlights approaching town, they had high-tailed it to the outskirts. At this hour, it didn't make sense for anyone else to be out on the roads. "Customs officers," they thought.

A faint glow that grew brighter as it neared pierced the black night. Harry Sokol—toting a lantern—had been sent to ease the visitors' minds and urge their return so they could get down to business.

"I'm one of the boys from the Liquor Exporters," Sokol told them.

The lights they had seen approaching town came from a vehicle carrying businessmen just like themselves. Sokol had accompanied two guys from Sioux City, Iowa, across the line from Minot on orders from Mr. Abner, the head manager. When they had pulled up to the office in Gainsborough sometime between one and two o'clock in the morning on November 22, 1920, Sokol heard how Eddie Norris and the other five men from Omaha, Nebraska, had skedaddled because they thought it was customs officers sniffing around. So Sokol and his lantern went to retrieve them.

Sokol jumped into the car next to Norris and Tom Kelly, and they headed back to Liquor Exporters Limited. Conveniently located next to the railway tracks that brought in the shipments, it was one in a line of Bronfman boozoriums dotting Canadian border towns.

When Sokol got inside the office, Eddie Norris was already wrangling with bookkeeper Jack Slusky over the price on the whiskey. As they negotiated, a couple of the Omaha crew wandered into the back, to the pantry where the loose liquor bottles from the broken cases were kept. Meanwhile, Tom Kelly was monkeying with the combination dial on the safe.

It was time to move these guys along, thought Slusky.

The men finally settled on a price for 69 cases. Slusky was handed $400 cash, and three cheques—for $2,000, $1,600, and $600. They were drawn on the State Bank of Andover in South Dakota. Suspicious, Slusky passed them to Paul Matoff to look over. Married to the sister of the big bosses, the Bronfman brothers, Matoff had been sent to Gainsborough about a month earlier to look after his brother-in-laws' business interests. He drew $50 a week for a position Matoff liked to call "the inside man."

"I know I've received quite a few cheques from Mr. Kelly," Matoff said, scanning the paper Slusky handed him.

Anxious to get moving, Norris assured the men he'd be responsible if the cheques were no good. Satisfied, Slusky stuffed them in his pocket and told Matoff to show the men down to Warehouse Number 2 to collect their booze. The boys who slept in the two warehouses minding the wares had already been roused to load the cars.

Sokol arrived a few minutes later to see the visitors helping themselves to cases of liquor stacked near the door.

"What are you trying to do?" he shouted.

"It's not your goddamned business," Kelly fired back.

But actually, it was. Sokol's unofficial title was clerk, but a few months earlier, he had bought into Liquor Exporters. So he had a personal stake in the money that was, at the moment, walking out the door. Each case held a dozen bottles. The liquor sold from the export house didn't go out in cases; it was transferred to burlap sacks for easy hauling by the bootleggers. But the booze Kelly and his men were toting out was still in cases. It clearly wasn't part of the deal.

As he grabbed at a case, Sokol yelled to Sam Rabinovitch, an employee loading the cars, "Can't you watch them? They were stealing whiskey."

Rabinovitch grumbled, "I don't have eyes in the back of my head."

About then, Sokol spotted Norris. "What are you trying to do?" said Sokol. "Are you doing the same thing?"

Norris asked what Sokol would do about it.

"What do you mean? I would stop you from taking it," Sokol replied. It was a pretty bold statement, considering Norris and the other five men had made no attempt to hide the revolvers on their hips or tucked into the belts on their pants. Lots of the guys coming from the States to buy booze carried guns.

Sokol ran the block and a half back to the office to tell Slusky what was going on. Upon his return to the warehouse, one of the Cadillacs had pulled out and the other was being loaded. The first car turned around, so Sokol hollered, "This is the road. It's not that road."

Seeing that the car had stopped, Sokol ran up. That's when he noticed the cases of liquor on the ground. "What are you trying to do?" he asked.

Kelly and another fellow jumped out with their guns, one in each hand.

"You better keep your mouth shut," came the reply, "or else we'll fill you full of lead."

It didn't take Sokol long to size up the odds—four guns to none. He shouted for help as he ran for the warehouse. Then he, Rabinovitch, and Mike MacDonald went back to the car. Sokol and MacDonald each grabbed one of the cases still on the ground while Rabinovitch bent down to pick up two.

The Americans accused them of stealing their booze. "No," Sokol replied, "we're trying to take our liquor."

As Rabinovitch was bent down, Norris hit him on the right shoulder with his revolver.

In all the excitement, Matoff thought he heard a man yell, "Let's rush the warehouse," and another say, "If anyone makes a move, we'll blow your brains out." Matoff tried to calm things down, suggesting that wasn't necessary. "It might bring very bad results," he pleaded.

He padlocked the warehouse door and dashed for the office. He knew Slusky was holding a lot of money. After grabbing the cash, the two made for the hotel, where they holed up for the night.

Sokol returned to the office, where his two Sioux City friends were still waiting. He jumped in their car and went for the police.

Meanwhile, Rabinovitch and MacDonald returned to the warehouse to find the door locked up tighter than a killer's lips. They set the liquor cases down on the platform and looked up to see Norris standing there, his two revolvers at the ready.

Rabinovitch would remember the gunman's threat for months to come: "You goddamned Jew. If you ever make a move, I will blow your fucking head off."

Kelly kicked the door, broke off the lock with the back of his revolver, and the gang moved inside, helping themselves. They packed their cars and sped off into the night.

The next morning, Matoff arrived back at the warehouse to find the door wide open, the lock on the ground, and the goods inside in disarray. He estimated some 40 cases of liquor had been stolen, about $2,000 worth of goods. And as it turned out, even most of the liquor they had purchased wasn't really paid for; the cheques were forgeries.

All of the Liquor Exporters' employees, including Matoff, were subpoenaed to testify at subsequent trials. They were clear about the events of that night, but a little coy about the nature of their business.

"Did the bulk of your sales go across the line?" a savvy defence lawyer asked Sokol. "I don't remember," he replied, trying to stay on the right side of the US prohibition laws. Asked if it was a common occurrence to load up cars in the middle of the night, Rabinovitch admitted it happened about once a week. But when it was suggested these fellows were smuggling booze across the 49th parallel, Rabinovitch said he only loaded up the cars. He didn't know where they were headed. "Why don't you be honest and say they were rumrunners?" asked defence lawyer Ed Clarke. "How did I know?" Rabinovitch replied.

By June 1922, the law had shut down export houses like the one in Gainsborough, but that didn't stop the flow of liquor across the border. The whiskey was shipped by rail via Bienfait, another border town, where it was unloaded and stored in the express office until Matoff arranged for its release to a customer.

Matoff, waiting since 9:00 p.m. on October 3, 1922, was beginning to think his customer wasn't coming. Hired to do the bagging and loading, the Zellickson brothers were about to head back to Estevan when they finally saw the lights from Lee Dellage's Cadillac pull up about two hours after he'd been expected. Later, they would wonder about the other automobile, the roadster with its headlights off, that they had seen following but had turned north instead of towards the train station where Dellage stopped.

The Zellicksons, Dellage, and CPR agent Colin Rawcliffe transferred the bottles from 110 cases—rye, gin, cognac, brandy, port, and cocktails—into sacks and loaded up Dellage's Cadillac and a truck belonging to another Bronfman business, Dominion Distributers. Matoff and Dellage moved inside the CPR station around 1:30 a.m. to a desk beneath the front windows to settle accounts. The two men had done deals several times before, but this load was one of the largest. Dellage had an underground room near the barn on his farm at Lignite, North Dakota, where he stashed his wares. He gave Matoff a cheque for $1,500 as well as $6,000 cash, bundled in packs of $500. As Dellage momentarily stepped outside on the train platform, Matoff counted the money a second time, certain there was too much money in one of the bundles.

The deal was almost concluded around two o'clock in the morning when blasts from a 12-gauge, sawed-off shotgun shattered the windows behind the men. "Put 'em up you sons of bitches," someone shouted.

The men loading the vehicles outside had scampered for cover when they saw five or six men rush from boxcars near the station. Then they heard the shots.

Matoff was hit in the back. The shot, fired from less than seven feet away, struck just above his right kidney and tore through his liver and intestines. "Run boys, they're shooting," he managed to utter before crumpling to the floor.

At the sound of shooting, Rawcliffe hastily retreated through a back door and headed upstairs. He returned minutes later to see Dellage cradling Matoff's head as the wounded man lay in the doorway.

"Speak to me," he pleaded. "Speak to me, Paul."

Rawcliffe told him Matoff was dead. At 35 years of age, he'd left behind a wife and two children.

"Good God. No," replied a distraught Dellage, only a year older than the dead man. The rumrunner stepped outside to the train platform but urged Rawcliffe to go back inside in case the shooter returned.

"Come on boys, let's get this booze away," shouted Dellage.

He jumped into his Cadillac and Jimmy LaCoste, a young man with a reputation for his pool-playing and driving prowess, hopped into the truck, intent on rapidly covering the 15 miles to the border. There was a sizeable load of bootlegged booze that was in jeopardy once the cops arrived.

In the end, a man's life, the liquor that police found stashed in a haystack across the border, $6,000 cash, and a large $400 diamond wrenched from Matoff's trademark tie pin were all lost. The killer, whomever he was, also got away. A solitary, unidentified figure was seen running along the platform after the shooting. He appeared to be carrying a smoking gun in his hand and a bundle of bills in his mouth.

Theories abounded—robbery, retaliation for testifying against the Gainsborough bandits, revenge for a bad batch of booze, or even blunder by taking out the wrong target. They remain only that—theories.

Matoff's murderer guarded his secret even better than a rumrunner conceals his booze.

Dellage was tried in Matoff's murder and acquitted. He was also tried twice for the robbery and ultimately acquitted after a hung jury at the first trial. In 1967, the owner of a Bienfait pool hall, operated out of Matoff's former boozorium, tore up the old wooden flooring to find the rusted barrel of a shotgun.

AN UNCOMMON CRIMINAL

Regina lawyer Harold Fisher leaned over to the man in the prisoner's box. Although he was no stranger to the law, Lee Dellage was utterly confused when the judge asked him to elect his mode of trial. He had no lawyer to speak on his behalf, and Fisher, who was in the courtroom on other matters, obliged with a whispered explanation to Dellage. The accused appreciated the free legal advice.

Dellage, a notorious bootlegger, had dodged a murder conviction that fall. But the long arm of the law wasn't ready to let go that easily. Police were certain Dellage was guilty of something; it was just a matter of having sufficient evidence to prove it. The charge this time was robbery. He maintained his innocence and a trial date was set.

With Dellage's case out of the way, the judge called the next one.

Fisher took his turn in the prisoner's box.

Until a few months earlier, he was a respected lawyer working in a prominent Regina firm. He lived at a good address, was a member of the local Elks Club, and played cricket with the Hamilton Rovers Club.

Now, Fisher stood on the other side of the law, an accused criminal. In that regard, the barrister was not so different from the bootlegger. Each was accused of helping himself to other people's money. But whereas a desperado like Dellage was accused of arming himself with a gun to steal, Fisher preferred a pen. It was less violent, and had proven more effective.

His victims—some of whom hadn't even learned to count yet—were certainly none the wiser. After all, he was picking the pockets of orphaned children. Well, not their pockets exactly. Rather, Fisher raided their trust accounts, the very ones he was supposed to safeguard.

It was a calculated crime. And when the amount missing totalled some $38,000—minus one lawyer—it all added up.

Fisher had taken a leave of absence from the firm of Mackenzie, Thom, Bastedo and Jackson in the summer of 1922. He and his wife sailed for Britain on what his acquaintances believed was a well-deserved vacation. For two months, he sent letters, extending his leave from the firm where he had worked for seven years. He sent word that if there were any inquiries about the orphans' accounts, he could be reached at Bristol, where he and his wife had taken up residence.

By that fall, there were plenty of questions. Norman Mackenzie, chief partner in the firm, was the provincial government's official guardian of infants, with a duty to protect and represent the interests of minors on wills, estates, and trust funds. Fisher had been in charge of administering those accounts. In the course of at least a year before his disappearance, the learned lawyer dictated letters stating the enclosed cheques were for the infant heirs. But then he destroyed the letters and pocketed the cheques. Fisher forged the name of the payee and deposited the cheque to his personal account, absconding with the children's money. He was gone four months before the first of the forgeries was discovered. Then the law moved against the lawyer, a warrant issued for his arrest under the Fugitive Offenders' Act.

He was practising law in Bromley, just outside of London, when he landed in court as a prisoner. Fisher had surrendered himself at the Bow Street police station in January 1923. The Canadian government sent a letter to urge denial of bail. Fisher was held in custody until he was turned over to Saskatchewan Provincial Police assistant commissioner W. R. Tracy, who escorted his prisoner back to Canada aboard the *Montrose*.

A crowd gathered at the Regina train station on March 15, 1923, in eager anticipation of the wanted man's return to the city, but a failure to make train connections in Montreal left the people waiting.

Fisher finally appeared in a Regina courtroom the next day as an accused criminal. Only two of the charges were read aloud, but at his preliminary hearing a couple of weeks later it took the clerk a full 41 minutes to read through the 65 charges of fraud, forgery, and theft. At a time when a fine pair of gentleman's shoes could be had for $12 or a new suit for $22 or a brand new nine-room house for under $10,000, Fisher had plundered a fortune of $31,760.80 from the orphans' accounts and pilfered an additional $9,338 from the firm that had paid him well—but seemingly not enough.

Almost every lawyer in the city was in court that Friday the 13th, April 1923, when Fisher pleaded guilty to everything. There was one notable absence. Norman Mackenzie, Fisher's former employer, who repaid the losses from the children's accounts with money from the law firm, stayed away.

Like many in that packed courtroom, Judge James Hannon wanted to know where the money had gone and why the promising young lawyer had taken it.

"I don't think it is an offence that stands explaining," Fisher replied. He had arranged for $11,000 to go back to the law firm by assignment of debts and mortgages. "I have given back what I could. There is no use promising to do more. Five dollars' worth of performance is worth a hundred dollars' intention. I have no wish to say where the money went or what led to my taking it."

He was, however, quick to say what he had not done with it. The judge said he had heard Fisher took the money to set his wife on "Easy Street for all time." She wasn't in court to see her lawyer-husband come to her defence. She had stayed behind with family in London.

"There are rumours that my wife is mixed up in this affair. It is wrong," Fisher replied. His otherwise-strong orator's voice faltered. He said nothing more.

Defence lawyer Percy Anderson pleaded for leniency for his client. He likened Fisher's crimes to "robbing Peter to pay Paul" as he stole from one account to cover up the theft in another. But the cover would only stretch so far.

Anderson said Fisher had shown such promise. The 37-year-old barrister would have risen high. "If a man does wrong, he should not be eternally damned. Fisher is a young man who could be of benefit to society when he gets out of prison and starts again." Anderson urged Hannon not to "crush all hope from him."

In his 14 years on the bench, the judge had never had such a painful task.

"I need not speak to you of the breach of trust or the way you threw away your fine opportunities," the judge told Fisher.

"You have struck a heavy blow at society. You didn't play the game according to the rules. You sinned against the honour and the dignity of the profession to which you belong. I am glad you have been brought back to answer the charges against you."

Fisher, the lawyer, couldn't help himself. He interrupted the judge to correct him. "I surrendered, Your Honour."

Undeterred, Hannon continued: "I shudder to think of the effect on young lawyers and young law students if they could say, 'Look at what Fisher did, and got away with it.'"

The lawyer-turned-criminal became a prisoner, sentenced to seven years with hard labour.

Calmly and quietly, Fisher walked back to his seat. He took his place beside Lee Dellage and the other common criminals.

HOODWINKED

To the thousands who gathered, it seemed almost magical, an ethereal glow illuminating the night sky. The blaze was visible for miles, even out in the countryside around Moose Jaw. The source stood near the western edge of Caribou Street. It was larger than life—105 feet tall with a cross-arm that measured 35 feet.

Estimates put the crowd that spring night in June 1927 at between seven and ten thousand. They arrived by train from Regina and in vehicles from all parts of the province—Prince Albert, North Battleford, Yorkton, and Indian Head. They even poured in from the United States, Manitoba, and Alberta. The crowd rallied around that burning cross and the men with their fiery speeches.

Like that cross, Pat Emoury was himself a bit larger than life. A smooth orator and a stylish dresser, the 50-year-old could work a crowd into a frenzy with his preaching about law and order, high moral standards, racial purity, and "saving Canada for Canadians."

Emoury described himself as an evangelist, although his official title was actually Kleagle for the Invisible Empire, Knights of the Ku Klux Klan of Kanada. As a Klan recruiter, it was his job to secure members, collect the "Klectoken" or "Kontributions," administer the oath of allegiance, and assist in building the organization in Saskatchewan.

The appointment was given to Emoury in a letter dated December 18, 1926, and signed "by my Imperial authority, King Kleagle, Province of Saskatchewan, Lewis A. Scott."

On the king's orders, Emoury went to work. He set up in a hotel in Moose Jaw, where he garnered the greatest following. But he also took his message on the road, preaching at Klan revival meetings in towns like Fort Qu'Appelle and Carlyle and filling halls in cities, including Saskatoon and Prince Albert. The crowd was so large at the Grand Theatre in Regina one night in July 1927 that some people were turned away. Emoury touted the benefits of the "great, Christian, benevolent, fraternal organization" that didn't discriminate on the basis of politics or religion—although, as he admitted, Jewish people were barred from joining, and no black man could get in unless his face was painted white. The Klan was not anti-Catholic, Emoury insisted, but rather pro-Protestant. He spoke in favour of "selection and restriction" of immigrants.

It was a message that people bought. Emoury boasted at the Regina meeting that the Klan had grown to 46,500 members in the province under the guidance of himself and the Scotts—Lewis and his son Harold.

For a $10 admission fee and three dollars for dues, almost anyone could join the Invisible Empire. There was also a ladies' group, for women whose husbands, fathers, brothers, or sons were Klan members. The women paid half as much. Emoury also extended honourary free memberships to ministers and other "people of influence" who could help attract more people.

Some of the Moose Jaw members began asking about getting a charter and a permanent home given their swelling numbers and coffers. Emoury suggested the bank account and membership needed to grow even more before the Klan's Imperial Palace in Toronto would grant more autonomy to the local unit. He recommended upping the fees to $25.

But soon Emoury and the Scotts were just as invisible as the Empire. And so were the Kontributions.

Pressed by some of his fellow Klansman in Moose Jaw, John Van Dyk, the Moose Jaw lodge's assistant secretary,

Wanted for Larceny

HUGH EMMONS
Alias H. E. EMERSON, alias EMORY or EMOURY

I hold a warrant for the arrest of the above named on a charge of theft of $1,313.00, the property of the Ku Klux Klan of Canada.

This man was for several months active in the city of Regina and the city of Moose Jaw, Saskatchewan, as an organizer for the Ku Klux Klan, and about August 27th, 1927, he disappeared from this city, failing to hand over to the Klan the above-mentioned sum of money collected by him for that organization.

He is believed to have come to this Province from South Bend, Ind., where he is alleged to have been at one time a saloon keeper. He is described as follows:

DESCRIPTION.
Hugh Emmons, alias H. E. Emmerson, alias Emory.

American; age, 50 years; 5 ft. 9 or 10 ins.; 225 lbs.; stout, corpulent build; fair complexion; blue eyes; clean shaven; grey hair dyed brown; round full face; speaks with a strong Southern American accent; stylish dresser.

This man may be accompanied by his wife and two daughters, age 12 years and 6 years, respectively.

Any assistance you may be able to give in the apprehension of the above named will be greatly appreciated.

MARTIN BRUTON,
Chief Constable.
City Police Headquarters, Regina,
CIRCULAR NO. 30.   Saskatchewan, Canada, Nov. 11, 1927

Wanted poster for Emmons, circa 1927. Source: Department of the Attorney General files, Saskatchewan Archives Board, R-321-file 12.6. 3.

went to police in mid-October. He swore out a complaint alleging Emoury had stolen $1,313 from the Klan. There had never been any audit of the money received, and the only bank accounts were Emoury's personal ones. So the figure of $1,313 was arrived at after adding up the 13 money orders Emoury had received, coupled with $422 in actual cash that Klan secretary J. Riddell had personally delivered to Emoury at the Champs Hotel in Regina on September 17, 1927. The next day, Emoury was gone.

Arrest warrants were issued for former saloon keeper Hugh "Pat" Emmons—alias H. E. Emerson, also known by the surname Emoury or Emory—and for Lewis and Harold Scott, who were wanted on fraud charges stemming from the Klan funds collected in Regina. A police informant put the total Klan membership in the province at around 10,280,

Police Headquarters,
Regina, Saskatchewan, Canada
Sept. 30, 1927

Wanted for False Pretences

I hold warrants for the apprehension of the following described men on several charges of obtaining money by means of false pretences. If located arrest and wire me.

LEWIS A. SCOTT

American; age 54 years; height 5 ft. 9 inches; weight 189 lbs.; stout build; broad, heavy shoulders; fair complexion; brown eyes; dark brown hair, trimmed very short, bald on top. Dresses very neatly, always wearing grey clothes and grey fedora hat, size 7 1/8; fluent talker and speaks in a very forcible manner; wears watch fob of elks tooth, and finger ring with emblem of The Order of the Eagles.

HAROLD L. SCOTT

American; age 37 years; height 5 ft. 9 in.; weight 170 lbs.; medium build; square shoulders; military appearance; sallow complexion; brown eyes; brown hair, thin on top; clean shaven; speaks with a distinct American accent, and has the habit of twisting his mouth to one side when talking. Usually wears grey clothes and grey fedora hat; is always accompanied by a female Boston bull-dog.

These men, who claim to be father and son, arrived in this city during the month of November, 1926, stating that they came from South Bend, Indiana, as organizers for Klu Klux Klan of Canada. They succeeded in enrolling a great number of candidates, collecting a fee from each candidate, the total amounting to thousands of dollars.

Both men disappeared from Regina on the 18th instant, taking all monies collected with them.

Any assistance you can give in the apprehension of these men will be much appreciated.

MARTIN BRUTON,
Chief Constable.

Wanted poster for the Scotts. Source: Regina Police Service museum.

and one officer estimated the trio had brought in roughly $87,000.

The law finally caught up to Emmons in February 1928 at his home in South Bend, Indiana. Many people, including Van Dyk, who had laid the complaint, assumed the American man would fight extradition.

Van Dyk was having second thoughts about informing on a fellow Klansman. Van Dyk had been a police officer in Moose Jaw until he was fired for his affiliation with the Klan. The man he knew as Emoury had taken him in and given him a job in the Klan's Moose Jaw office. Van Dyk wrote to his old friend on March 27, 1928, addressing his letter "Dear Pop."

"I wanted to talk to you about that warrant," Van Dyk wrote. "It was not my fault that it was sworn out. A whole bunch of them got together and made me do it. You do not need to be afraid. I am under no consideration to prosecute you." Van Dyk hoped the Klan leader could help again. "Would you ask

Hugh Pat Emmons, 1928. Reproduced with permission from Regina *Leader–Post.*

Governor Jackson if there is any chance to get on as a motorcycle policeman, because if I do not get something quick I will starve to death."

Van Dyk didn't get work in the States; and he didn't starve. By the time Emmons, who didn't fight extradition, arrived back in Regina for his trial, Van Dyk was the police chief in Melville. On the witness stand, he was reluctant to name names about exactly which Klansman had urged him to have Emmons charged.

Among the Crown's witnesses was Regina accountant J. W. Rosborough, the Imperial Wizard of the Invisible Empire of the Knights of the Ku Klux Klan, head of the

Saskatchewan organization. He had begun to ask questions about the collected money—and wasn't satisfied with the answers.

Pat Emoury was actually Hugh Finley Emmons, who had been Exalted Cyclops in the Indiana Ku Klux Klan until January 1927. The jowly faced, rotund Cyclops was also known by the name Pat—a derivative of his nickname Fat. Like many Klansman in Indiana, Emmons had parted with the group after its Grand Dragon was convicted of the abduction, rape, and murder of a schoolteacher.

Taking the witness stand in a Regina courtroom in May 1928, Emmons was like a preacher in the pulpit with a full house. The ex-Exalted Cyclops waxed eloquent as he talked about his vision for a new Klan in Canada. Emmons said he had been reluctant to come back into the fold until convinced by Lewis Scott, also from Indiana, who assured him they would help build "a good clean Christian, beneficent organization. They will not have the whipping crew or tar and feathering or stuff like we had in the States."

In fact, claimed Emmons, Scott had suggested the name change—to distance them from the Klan scandal in Indiana, where Emmons had testified at Senate hearings into allegations of bribery and corruption.

Pressed by prosecutor Herbert Sampson about some of the statements Emmons had made during his Saskatchewan speeches, he insisted that he had never suggested he was a Canadian.

"I said I was born south of Toronto in my lectures," Emmons said with his southern drawl. "I did not say how far south. I said I was born south of Toronto, and I said I am a good Canadian." He had been equally murky about the actual number of Klansman, having given numbers ranging from 9,000 to 48,000 at various meetings.

But Emmons was very clear about one thing: "I did not steal $1,313," he told the court. Emmons testified that he had agreed to become Kleagle on the condition that he would get eight dollars of every membership in Moose Jaw. The other five dollars was to go to the King Kleagle, Scott. But in April 1927, Emmons contacted Scott and said he needed more, so the amount grew to the full $13 for everyone who joined in Moose Jaw. As well, he received two dollars for each person who signed up after one of his lectures elsewhere. He could also pocket the money from the women's branch. The Scotts had the same arrangement for money collected in Regina.

And Emmons had the paperwork to back up his claims, producing several letters signed by the King Kleagle. "I am sure glad to tell you now that everything in Toronto was OK. I had a conference with Mr. C. L. Fowler. ... He has agreed to let me have all monies collected in Moose Jaw and Regina so as to get things moving in the province," Lewis Scott had reportedly written to Emmons in May 1927. Fowler had become the Klan's Imperial Wizard in Canada after being ousted from the organization and his church in the States. The letters were embossed with an official-looking seal—a cross circled by the words "Invisible Empire, Knights of the Ku Klux Klan, Saskatchewan."

Emmons estimated there were 2,000 Klansmen in Moose Jaw, and he personally took in as much as $20,000. But, he noted, he had to pay for office and meeting expenses from that money. He said he left with no more than about $1,650 extra in his pocket.

As for his seemingly hasty departure, Emmons said he had become disenchanted with the Klan because politicians had "snatched" it out of his hands. He had sought his leave from the King Kleagle a day after collecting the money from Riddell. Emmons had a letter to back that up too, releasing him and the Scotts since a new man was taking over. It also gave Emmons a bonus of two dollars per head for anyone who joined after his departure until January 1928.

The Scotts were unavailable to actually vouch for Emmons or the letters. Emmons heard they had headed to Australia to get the Klan going there. "They asked me to go, but I washed my hands forever of the Klan," he said, stretching out his hands for those in the court to see. "See, they are clean."

Clean, perhaps, but not lily-white. Faced with evidence that seemed to give Emmons the right to keep all the money that—as Magistrate J. H. Heffernan put it—the "the suckers who were gathered in paid to the order," the judge had to acquit. But Heffernan certainly believed Saskatchewan people had been hoodwinked by the American Klansman.

"They have had the audacity to tell us what the Union Jack stands for. Imagine a few Canadians going over to the United States and starting in on a campaign to tell the people what their flag stands for and what the Constitution of the United States means. They would be tarred and feathered and rolled out of town."

Emmons was also acquitted days later in Moose Jaw on a charge of fraudulently taking $6.50 from Margaret Wilkinson, who had joined the women's Klan group. However, the evidence showed she had signed her membership at the urging of her husband, not Emmons.

"The surprising feature of the disclosures made at this trial is that men who were members of the organization made dupes not only of themselves, but also allowed their wives and even their mothers to fall into the same deceptive net," Magistrate Loy Sifton concluded.

Despite all the revelations about the wizards behind the magic, the myths, and the money, the Invisible Empire would not disappear from Saskatchewan for several more years.

PRAIRIE CHICKENS

The gun was unusual, a cross between a rifle and a shotgun. The smaller barrel was used for shooting larger game. James Alak mostly used the shotgun for taking down prairie chickens. His neighbour Andy Ader had helped him fix the stock on the gun the previous winter.

It was nearing the end of summer when James went hunting. Spotting the prey in his farmyard, he lifted his combination rifle-shotgun and fired. When he returned later, after shooting the other two, he found his intended target was wounded, but not dead. James fired again, this shot on the side below the ribs, at close range, just to be sure.

He caught the second one on the run. James gave chase through the fields, felling his prey with a single blast from about 30 feet away.

Walking northwest across the prairie fields, James covered about two miles before he again took aim. His first shot missed. But the next two found their mark.

When he came upon the baby, now alone, James paused. It didn't seem right to leave the motherless creature; but then, it didn't seem right to end her life, either. James took pity and walked away. And he kept on walking.

He was still cradling the gun when he arrived at Andy's house, the same neighbour who had helped James with the stock. And now, James wanted Andy's assistance once again. Using the weapon as a table, James placed a piece of paper on the stock and scribbled a note to his mother, still in Hungary.

He wanted Andy to send it to her, to let her know he wasn't coming back.

James later couldn't recall exactly how many shots he had fired that day, but he remembered using the larger barrel, the shotgun—"what I shoot prairie chickens with."

Except this time James had killed his family: First his father-in-law, Luke Bugyik; then Theresa, Luke's daughter and James's wife; and ultimately his mother-in-law, Elizabeth, who died of her wounds in a Saskatoon hospital five days after James hunted her down in her farmhouse. He fired once through the window and missed. She ran to another room, but he got her in the abdomen. She tried to run, but a third shot stopped her.

James spared the toddler, even though he was convinced he hadn't fathered the girl born nine months after James had married Theresa.

When he arrived at his neighbour's farm, James wasn't finished. He had one more kill to make.

"I need to die," James said. He had twisted a piece of binder twine onto the trigger. He could pull it with his toe.

* * *

James Alak and Theresa Bugyik had married in November 1909. She left him three weeks later, a victim of abuse. She moved away to Moose Jaw, where she gave birth to her daughter on August 5, 1910. That same month, Theresa moved back home—reunited with her parents and brother, Luke Jr., on the family farm near Vanscoy.

James followed two weeks later and insisted, with his revolver, that she return to his house. She declined.

"He said then if she didn't come back, somebody would have to die that day," Luke Jr. would remember. Then James challenged his father-in-law to step outside and fight. Luke Jr. held his father back. James had drawn his revolver and was taking aim. When the old man didn't step outside, James left.

He came back the next summer, in July. This time, Theresa and the baby left with him. Determined to make a life with the man she had married, she took her furniture, household items, and a cow. Some chickens and a pig, gifts from her parents, would follow. It was a Monday when she went back to James—and it was a Monday, September 11, 1911, when she left him again to return to her family's farm.

James showed up the next day, demanding Theresa come back. Her brother, Luke, told James she didn't want to return to the man who was hurting her and threatening everyone else around her. Even if the police couldn't prove it, Luke blamed James for the mysterious fires that had destroyed the Bugyiks' hay bales and barn. James told Luke it would kill him if Theresa didn't come home.

The wagon pulled into James's yard that afternoon.

Theresa and her father had come to pick up her goods. They had Andy Ader with them to lend a hand. Mr. Bugyik hauled out the bed. Theresa packed up her dishes. Andy carried out a trunk that was too heavy for Theresa's father and added it to the growing load in the back of the wagon. The whole time, James was pleading with Theresa's father not to take her away.

"If you would behave like you did for a little while after she came back, it would be all right, she would be staying with you instead of going away," Mr. Bugyik told James. But he couldn't behave and she wouldn't stay. She wanted a divorce.

With the wagon nearly packed, Theresa headed towards the barn to gather up the chickens. Her father remained behind to tie the cow to the wagon. James asked Andy to join him so they could help Theresa with the chickens. But when Andy got to the far side of a bluff of trees, he could no longer see James.

Theresa had just finished tying up the second sack of chickens when she and Andy heard the shot. They ran for the house.

They saw the wagon with her father slumped against the wheel. Andy stopped to help him as Theresa ran past, into the fields.

Fearing the cow might step on the wounded old man, Andy dragged him clear of the wagon. Blood was pouring from the left side of Bugyik's head. He waved his hands back and forth, unable to say anything. Andy looked up to see James running, the shotgun-rifle in his hand. Andy jumped in front of the gunman, asking what James was doing. There was no reply. Dodging Andy, James continued to chase his frantic wife.

Andy heard the blast and saw Theresa fall forwards onto the ground.

Fearing James might turn on him, Andy too had fled, running the half mile to his home to protect his family. Andy believed James had come to kill him when he showed up with the letter for his mother in Hungary. That's when Andy learned that James had also critically wounded Elizabeth Bugyik. James said he was going back to his wife. Parted in life, they would lie together in death when he used the binder twine to pull the trigger on his gun.

When Andy urged him to turn himself in to police instead of taking his life, James said he didn't want anybody to make him suffer.

Then James left for home.

* * *

When Martin Ryder saw the double-barrelled shotgun-rifle, it was propped up in the corner behind the table, inside James's house. The Royal Northwest Mounted Police constable had been on the train from Saskatoon, heading back to Kindersley, when he saw the crowd of people gathered on the railway platform at Vanscoy. He thought it best to get off and find out what was going on. He was taken by car to the Bugyiks' house, where he found neighbours trying to assist the older woman who had been shot in the back.

Ryder drove to James's house and found the body of the old man in a pool of blood near the wagon, the cow still tied to the back. Ryder went looking for Theresa, but instead found the gun used to kill her. An empty cartridge lay nearby on the floor, and two full cartridges were on the table.

Ryder looked again for Theresa's body in the moonlight and finally found her. She had made it about one hundred yards from the house before she was felled by her husband's gun, shot in the back, the pellets spraying and leaving nine wounds.

Ryder had neighbours lay the bodies out on the kitchen table in the house where Theresa had never felt at home.

* * *

Word of the shootings had reached the Mounties in Saskatoon. Three officers were in a democrat wagon on their way to Vanscoy when, about five miles from their destination, they spied another wagon approaching in the twilight. It seemed awfully late for a farmer to be out.

The wagon came to a stop in front of the democrat.

"A serious thing has happened," James said.

He had not used his shotgun-rifle to kill himself; he had heeded Andy's advice to turn himself in to police.

While awaiting his fate in a Prince Albert jail cell, James wrote a letter to the Austrian-Hungarian consulate, pleading for assistance to spare his life. He also wrote in Hungarian to the justice minister and to King George V. "I am very penitent and would ask your pardon," James scrawled in black ink across cream-coloured paper. In a postscript he added that he had also written to the Hungarian king.

The consul-general of Austria-Hungary responded. He sent an inquiry to the Canadian government, indicating receipt of James's letter and asking to intercede on his behalf. The letter was dated February 7, 1912, and it was too late.

On November 27, 1911—10 days after what would have been his second wedding anniversary—James was hanged, a gruesomely slow, unmerciful hanging. The man who feared suffering, who moaned audibly as he mounted the steps to the scaffold, hanged for a full 13 minutes, dying of strangulation, not of a quick snap of the neck.

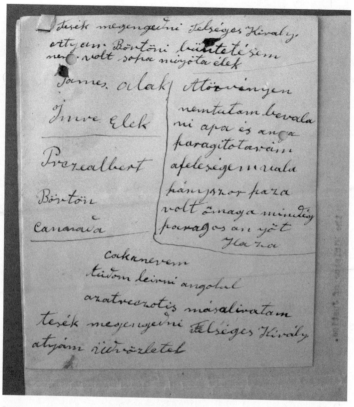

Letter written in prison by James Alak. Source: Department of Justice fonds, Library and Archives Canada, RG 13, Vol. 1460.

The letter James had sent to Austria had instead gone to Australia. Recognizing the mix-up, someone in Australia had then forwarded it to its rightful destination, where it arrived nearly two months after James's death.

In its reply to the consul-general's belated letter, the Canadian government explained that the case had been carefully considered, and there was nothing to recommend commuting of the death sentence in any event.

"His crime was a very atrocious one," the justice minister replied.

Theresa shares a grave with her father.

OF MEN AND MADNESS

As the reporter enters barracks square, he sees the red-coated men on the veranda of the guardroom. There is a much heavier guard, he notes, and is told 42 mounts are minding 68 prisoners. The Rebellion has caused a lot of problems, not the least of which is trying to hold that many prisoners at the North-West Mounted Police barracks in Regina. Some of the prisoners are detained in tents.

Another cell will be empty soon enough.

The reporter has come to see the hanging. But that will come later.

Stepping inside the prison, he sees a number of the policemen are still at breakfast. The prisoner, a powerfully built, dark-haired man with a round face and deep blue eyes, is in the cell immediately behind them.

"There is," says the prisoner, "no use in asking questions." He is talking to the Reverend Urquhart, not the reporter. The clergyman is trying to urge the condemned man to clear his conscience in the time left to him.

"We are all friends," cries the prisoner. The reporter believes the man is feigning madness. At this point, insanity might be the only way to spare the prisoner's life.

"The Indian is a friend of mine. He is innocent too. I was 99 degrees in the other world, that is the degree. Wait and I will explain it," the man imprisoned behind the grate says.

"Before God, you all have to appear. When a man is innocent, I don't care who denies it," he says, then laughs. "I will explain it here. As a man sits in a dark cell. Now you have to give him a table and give him means and enough for his family and enough for his friends and enough for every one. That is all I want."

Urquhart and the jailer, Richard Deane, try again to speak to him. "Don't ask me any questions," he says, waving impatiently. "I was laying in my cell. I wanted to go to my place and sit down and eat and drink. Nothing at all. Dr. Jukes—Captain Deane and the Doctor, my two friends."

Urquhart consults with the doctor. The senior surgeon for the Mounted Police, Dr. A. Jukes, has already given his report, pronouncing John Connor of sound enough mind to be executed. The reverend tries once more to reach out to Connor.

"Don't talk to me anymore. No more talk. Good-bye," he replies with his heavy German accent. "My trust was in God and then in the Doctor. But God is Captain Deane and then the Doctor. I don't want any questions and I don't want you to bother me anymore."

It is eight o'clock in the morning. Those who will witness the death ascend a stairway leading to the floor above the cells, where the drop and the rope have been prepared. The prisoner passes through a double file of officers, and his arms are pinioned. Once he's led to the trap door, his legs are strapped together and the noose slipped around his neck.

"Have you anything to say before sentence of death is carried out on you?" the executioner asks.

Silence.

* * *

William Hannah saw the flash of lantern light moving from front to back in the shanty house. He wondered what John Connor could be doing at this hour. It was nearing midnight on Sunday, and Hannah, on duty in the nearby Canadian Pacific Railway roundhouse in Moose Jaw, thought it odd

Connor would be up so late. But stranger yet were the sounds he heard closer to morning, around four or five o'clock. From the roundhouse, some three hundred yards away from the shanty, it sounded like chopping and scraping wood.

"I wonder what Connor is about so early?" Hannah muttered to the others in the roundhouse.

On Tuesday afternoon, April 7, 1885, NWMP Constable Alexander Henderson was walking on the foot trail along the south bank of the Moose Jaw Creek when he saw the corpse—or more precisely an arm, a chest, and two knees. On closer inspection, Henderson saw the dead man was naked except for a shirt and undershirt drawn up over his face and outstretched hands, and an iron logging chain wrapped around his neck and torso. Partially frozen, the body lay on its back on top of the ice-covered creek, about three yards from shore. It was caked in about an inch of ice from water that had melted, then frozen again.

It took several men, a team of horses, a rope, and a ladder to get the body from the creek onto the land. Using a spade, the teamster broke the ice to free the body so it could be put on the ladder and hauled up the high, steep bank, where a crowd of about 20 people waited. Before the rigid body was placed in the back of the wagon, the teamster tore open the shirt to see if the corpse had a familiar face.

They stared at Henry Mulaski.

As the shirt was drawn open, blood began to ooze from the wounds on Henry's neck, head, and face. The worst of the blows had severed his right ear.

Police would see more blood that night—inside Connor's house. It was on the floor, bed, and walls of the 16- by 12-foot shack. One particularly large pool was covered partly by a carpet. The stove still held cinders of burnt clothing as well as a few buttons and two buckles, like those used on waistcoats and trousers. A shirt and a woollen sock with red stains were in the trunk. It also kept a pair of moleskin trousers, from which the front part of the legs had been cut or torn away—but not enough to get rid of one stubborn red spot. The straw

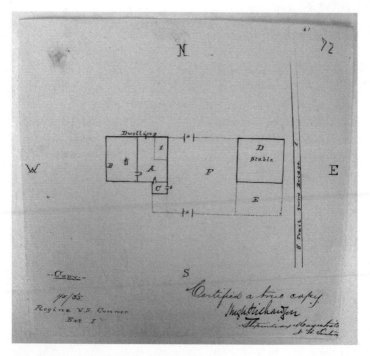

Map of the crime scene in the Connor case. Source: Department of Justice fonds, Library and Archives Canada, RG 13, Vol. 1421.

tick was missing from the bed. It was in the corral, where blood-stained straw had been scattered.

Sergeant Jeremiah Fyfe found the axe inside the porch. The wooden handle was broken, the pieces left on the woodpile.

A trail of bloodstains in the grass and shrubbery led Fyfe from the house to the bank of the Moose Jaw Creek.

Mulaski had arrived in Moose Jaw on the Sunday train from Chaplin. He'd spent the last few weeks working for the CPR, earning $1.50 a day digging ditches and paying four dollars a week for board. He collected $14.40 pay that Sunday, and said he was heading for his homestead. When he left the railway station, he had a gun in one hand—bought with some of his earnings—and a parcel of clothes in the other.

Immigrants from the old country who had come to build a railroad and a new life, Mulaski, a Pole, had lived with

Connor, a German Jew, on and off for a couple of years. They were on friendly terms—or so everyone thought.

Connor was out working with his team of horses when Fyfe came to arrest him. "That's the first time I heard of the murder," Connor told the officer.

Three weeks later, Connor went on trial, accused that he did "feloniously, wilfully and of his malice aforethought, kill and murder one Henry Mulaski."

Connor told the coroner the logging chain wrapped around the dead man appeared to be his. Prosecutor David Scott insisted that admission, and a chain of circumstantial evidence linking Connor to the crime, was enough to wrap a noose around the prisoner's neck. But where, defence lawyer Thomas Johnstone asked, was the evidence of a quarrel between the two friends?

Testifying for the defence, Catherine Buckley said she had seen Mulaski at the Presbyterian church in Moose Jaw that Sunday. Connor, who was sweet on Catherine, was also there. He accompanied her home, staying until almost 9:30 that night, when he left with three loaves of freshly baked bread, a gift from Catherine's mother.

Connor had told the coroner Mulaski was already asleep when he got home. He climbed into bed next to his roommate. When he awoke Monday morning, Mulaski was gone. He remembered that his friend seemed scared of the war raging to the north.

He also recalled that Mulaski had given him $13 to pay for a pony purchased from an Indian man.

Mush-Ta-Sea, a Sioux Indian, testified through an interpreter. But he wasn't much help to Connor. Mush-Ta-Sea said he knew the prisoner, but had never been to his house and didn't know anything about a recent horse trade.

Johnstone tried to argue it was Mush-Ta-Sea who had killed Mulaski during the transaction involving the horse. Scott cried foul at the defence lawyer's attempt to give evidence when his client had never taken the stand.

The jurors didn't buy it anyway. They reached a guilty verdict in less than an hour.

Before he was sentenced, Connor spoke of his former life, how he had mastered several languages during his three years in Canada, and of his friendship with Mulaski. Finally, he accused Mush-Ta-Sea of the murder.

Judge Hugh Richardson had the final word. He sentenced Connor to die.

* * *

The trap door swings open. But Connor does not fall to his death. The condemned man "writhed in agony," the Regina *Daily Leader* reporter records on July 17, 1885. After five minutes, Dr. Henry Dodd goes down and feels Connor's pulse.

"Pulse still beats," he says. "A strong man."

Connor's legs quiver, so Dr. Dodd puts his ear to the man's chest. "The heart still beats," he says. "It is purely muscular action." Dr. Jukes checks as well and finds a pulse at the wrist.

Chief Stewart and another policeman wonder whether the fall was deep enough. Someone notices that Connor's head leans back a little and the knot on the noose is almost under the chin, instead of where it should be, beneath the left ear to ensure a snapped neck. The 25-year-old tortuously strangles. After nine minutes of hanging, doctors confirm his heartbeat has ceased.

"It's a ghastly sight which sickened strong men," the reporter writes.

The next day's newspaper carries an editorial titled "Hanging as a Fine Art." It muses about prejudice against the hangman's trade, adding "the real hangman is Parliament or the people ... Why be down on the man who adjusts the fatal necktie?" It goes on at length with gallows humour, but then concludes, "Our knowledge on this sublime subject is exhausted. We shall add to our staff ... Thanks to the spirited support we get from our patrons, we shall add to this a hanging editor, and then look out for a long, learned treatise on the interesting subject of the happy despatch."

Telegram sent in 1885 confirming Connor's execution. Source: Department of Justice fonds, Library and Archives Canada, RG 13, Vol. 1421.

The same day Connor dies, the newspaper runs a full transcript of the formal charging of another dark-haired prisoner held in the same jail as Connor. It's dated July 6 before Judge Richardson, the magistrate who also presided at Connor's trial, and begins, "Louis Riel—do you hear me?"

"Yes, your Honour," he replies. In four months, the condemned man will swing from the same gallows that witnessed Connor's bungled dispatch. A reporter disguised as a priest will visit the Métis leader in his cell the night before his date with the hangman. As with Connor, some will question the prisoner's sanity.

He is prepared for death, Riel tells the reporter. "But yet the Spirit tells me, told me last night, that I should yet rule a vast country, the North West, with power derived direct from heaven," he says. "The spirit speaks, Riel will not die until he has accomplished his mission."

* * *

More than a century and a quarter later, a journalist lifts open the lid on a small cardboard box of court archives in Ottawa. She is surprised to discover that the manila folder marked John Connor, a man largely forgotten by history, is filed immediately next to the one that reads: Louis Riel.

FREE RANGE

The title wasn't exactly catchy. The book was called *Mathematical Techniques to Assist in Balancing and Formulating Human Diets with Natural Nutrient Sources*. Weighty by name but slim in size at just 82 pages, *Mathematical Techniques* wasn't simply another diet book advocating a protein-rich, low-carb diet. Rather, it reduced choosing good nutrition to a mathematical certainty.

"Anything we can do to encourage people to be on track in their nutrient intake is good," author Ken Kettleson told *Moose Jaw Times-Herald* reporter Ron Walter for a profile of the coil-bound book in September 2005.

Ten months later, Kettleson vanished.

And he was not a person who was easy to lose. A large man at 220 pounds and four inches shy of six feet, Kenneth Carl Angus Kettleson had a heavy, thick full beard and moustache that matched his greying, reddish-brown, medium-length hair. He looked like a character from the 1970s television show *The Life and Times of Grizzly Adams*. In fact, he used to tell people that he sometimes visited a bear's den on the land around his farm, south of Moose Jaw. Kettleson had been a hunter for most of his life, and still bore the scar on his stomach where he had accidentally shot himself at age 16 or 17 while removing a gun from a closet. An avid outdoorsman with a proficiency in local plant life and a passion for hiking, Kettleson's trademark outfit was comprised of his black pants, black shirt, khaki zipper vest with plenty of pockets to collect things, wide-brimmed, light-coloured canvas hiking hat, and brown ankle boots made for walking.

Yet, Dr. Kettleson, who wore thick glasses, was as much at home roaming the halls of academia as he was wandering the countryside. He topped off a bachelor of science degree in agriculture with a master of science in nutrition from McGill University, and, in 1986, added a Ph.D. in animal nutrition from Texas A&M.

As he told Walter, his primary reason for heading to Texas for his doctoral studies was its coyote-rich environment. He wanted to examine a non-lethal means of stopping coyotes from killing sheep and goats. But his focus of study ended up shifting to the potential toxicity of aluminum and other minerals.

It was a different toxic chemical that Kettleson relied upon in his defence on an animal neglect charge. After his university studies in the States, he had eventually returned home. His parents, Carl and Charlotte, ran a large-scale cattle operation near Crestwynd, which Kettleson inherited in the mid-1990s after the couple passed away.

The RCMP and the Society for the Prevention of Cruelty to Animals took a keen interest in Kettleson's farm in 1997. He first contacted the Mounties in November 1996 because his dog was missing. Kettleson worried someone might have shot it for revenge, contending some people in the area didn't like his free-range "porkers." He thought a few of his calves might be missing too.

About a week later, a Mountie and SPCA investigator David Long visited the ranch. Cattle stood along the road as they entered the yard. Pigs of varying ages roaming the property ran up to greet them. Kettleson pulled on a coat, poured piles of food pellets in the snow for the pigs, then gave Long and the officer a tour. He spoke with affection for his animals. In addition to about a hundred head of cattle, Kettleson had some 30 pigs that he called by name. (Earlier that winter, he had butchered a hog named Pork Chops for a friend.) As they walked, Kettleson, the academic, expounded at length on his research studies about how livestock should be allowed to roam and thrived when sheltered on natural floors for warmth. Long, who questioned the wisdom of keeping the animals in an old, unheated shed, told Kettleson to ensure he had enough feed and bedding for the animals through what was shaping up to be a bitterly cold winter.

In early January, Long got a call from Kettleson after four of his pigs had died. He suspected poison. Long helped dig the carcasses out of a snowbank and took them to a lab. Kettleson called again a short time later, convinced that still more of his pigs had been poisoned to death.

"Ken told me he was worried for his own life," Long would testify in 1998 at Kettleson's trial. "He said that if these people were poisoning his pigs, it wouldn't be much of a stretch for them to come and do away with him." Kettleson believed people wanted him dead so they could take his land.

A veterinarian pathologist concluded the pigs had died from starvation. No tests were run for poison, but he didn't see any physical signs of it.

The Mounties and the SPCA moved in to seize Kettleson's livestock on a frigid day in late January 1997. Most of the cattle and pigs were huddled together inside the unheated shed without feed, water, or bedding. The floor was covered at least a foot deep in a soupy mix of urine, manure, and mud. There was one dead pig in the muck and another, near death, trapped sideways in the mess. Long put down the pathetic, badly injured animal.

Many of the 16 pigs were overly thin, their skin stretched across easily visible rib, hip, and shoulder bones. Their hair had grown long and straggly, another sign of their malnourished state. And some seemed to have lesions on their skin, as if frostbitten. The cattle were not nearly as bad.

The trial became a case of duelling scientists. Two vets who had visited the farm with Long concluded the care Kettleson had provided for the animals was insufficient. Then defence lawyer Charlene Richmond put her expert on the stand. The Edmonton toxicologist had tested samples cut from dead pigs in Kettleson's yard. One of the neighbours had noticed that the coyotes seemed to steer clear of the carcasses. And the local vet, who helped collect the samples, thought they didn't rot as usual, instead looking as though they'd been preserved. "It's like they were almost embalmed," he told the court.

The toxicologist found the samples contained the chemicals para-cresol—a wood preservative—and phenol. Used in an array of products from disinfectant to embalming fluid, the phenol was very highly concentrated. If it had been ingested, the concentrated, corrosive chemical likely would have caused burns inside the animal's throat and belly unless diluted. However, he thought the most likely explanation was that the chemical had been rubbed on the animals' skins. At that concentration, the phenol would have caused lesions—kind of like the ones the vets had blamed on frostbite. Animals exposed to phenol or para-cresol usually lose weight because they lose their desire to drink water.

But Judge David Orr was unconvinced by most of the evidence. The necropsy had found no lesions inside the bodies of the dead pigs. "I find it not only implausible, but inconceivable that (phenol) was in their drinking water," he said, noting that the water supply for the roaming pigs was snow.

"In addition to that, the idea that in the dark of night in this very heavily snowed-in yard where the pigs all ran completely at large all the time, that mysterious assailants got in, caught the animals and applied phenol to their skin, that idea strikes me as so outlandish as to be virtually impossible," said Orr. He went further, concluding the pigs had been starved to death.

"I think to accept the idea that they were poisoned is almost to be drawn into delusions which Dr. Kettleson had in his mind, and they clearly were delusions to me," said Orr. However, he found Kettleson honestly believed the emaciation was caused by poisoning and not his care, so didn't find criminal neglect in the animals' starvation. However, he did find the condition of the sheds "bizarrely inappropriate and clearly dangerous" for the pigs—adding up to Kettleson's guilt on that element of the charge.

The judge asked if Kettleson intended to keep livestock any more.

"Due to the presence, the unexplained, so to speak, presence of phenol in the tissues ...," Kettleson replied, "I cannot have animals again on the ranch until this problem is resolved."

He hired a private investigator, who spent two years looking for proof of the poison. Kettleson even took the battle to a higher court, but failed in a bid to overturn his conviction. He was originally fined, but, on appeal, that penalty was replaced by a conditional discharge with two years' probation. One of the conditions barred him from keeping any animals, except the dog and cats he then had, for the duration of the order.

The scientist-rancher remained convinced of his innocence and the phenol's guilt. "You can have a totally healthy animal," Kettleson told Walter while promoting the book about good nutrition, six years after the trial. "You give it phenol and it will die."

* * *

Kettleson's dogs first alerted his friends that something was amiss.

When his mail started to pile up at a Moose Jaw postal outlet in mid-July, 2006, store owner Jim Carr, who had known Kettleson for years, drove out to the farm. After his conviction, Kettleson never again raised cattle, letting the family's registered CK brand expire in 1998. He sold the farm to help finance his private investigation into the poisonings and to provide a means to live. The buyer allowed Kettleson to continue residing there. When Carr pulled into the farmyard, he found only two emaciated dogs that looked like they hadn't eaten in days. It was odd since Kettleson was known to take good care of the dogs. The visitor fed the animals and left.

Aerial view of Kettleson farm. Courtesy of the RCMP.

Because of Carr's inquiries, another friend drove out to the farm and was equally baffled by what he didn't see. Kettleson's pickup truck was parked outside the house, but its owner was nowhere to be found. The friend checked again the next day, then called police.

The Mounties arrived on July 15 to find the house locked up tightly, although the key Kettleson usually kept hidden was missing. When officers broke open the door, they discovered a house cluttered with clothing, books, and mounds of other items covered with dust and debris that betrayed Kettleson's reclusive lifestyle. A sleeping bag, a flashlight, and a large knife were on the middle of the floor in the living room that had become a makeshift bedroom. Beside the sleeping area was a prescription filled June 16. Kettleson had recently been diagnosed with high blood pressure. What police didn't find was the home's occupant or anything to suggest he had met with foul play.

Almost a month had passed since anyone had seen the 58-year-old. Kettleson had stopped by a friend's house on June 19 to pick up a single-shot, .22-calibre Winchester rifle, which, like Kettleson, has never surfaced despite extensive searches on land and by air.

The learned author of *Mathematical Techniques*—who knew his pigs by name, liked to roam pastures counting cattle out loud, swam in dugouts, enjoyed walking nude on his property, and ate raw wild meat—was never seen again.

And nothing added up.

THE SCISSORS GRINDER

The body would have been nearly impossible to identify. There was so little of it left, for one thing, the face only a mass of crawling worms by the time it was discovered under a stack of railway ties piled neatly in a grassy field outside town one June day in 1893. The dead man wasn't from around there, and there were so many travellers in those days it was impossible to remember them all.

Still, people somehow knew it was the scissors grinder.

The tailor, Daniel McCormick, remembered the scissors grinder by the holes in his pants—striped trousers that were too short and patched with multicoloured fabric. James Hood, the shoemaker from Moose Jaw, remembered the boots—heavy and broad-toed, finished with Hungarian nails.

And nearly everybody remembered the machine, that strange contraption the scissors grinder had worn on his back. It was a big homemade thing fashioned from an emery stone and the wheel from a baby carriage.

North-West Mounted Police Sergeant Jeremiah Fyfe had seen the scissors grinder in Regina earlier that month and then again in Fort Qu'Appelle a few days later. The contraption caught the officer's attention on both occasions.

When Fyfe saw the decomposing body outside town, something called the scissors grinder immediately to mind, though his machine was nowhere to be found.

* * *

The body was discovered by farmer John Shaw, whose attention had been caught by a swarm of flies on the road outside Grenfell. When he followed the swarm, Shaw saw human toes sticking out from underneath a pile of railway ties in the grass, and immediately went to get help.

It was a gruesome scene. Lying for weeks in the prairie sun and heat, the body had been reduced in places to bones, and decomposition was severe everywhere else. In the pockets of the man's tattered striped pants was $5.15 wrapped up in a hanky. There weren't any other signs of who the man may have been, his only belongings the clothes he was wearing.

What happened to him was equally mysterious.

There had obviously been a campfire, but there was no sign of a wagon or horses, and there were no other obvious clues at the scene. Police commissioned Sangwish, an Indian tracker, to help with the investigation.

Standing in the long grasses near where the body was found, Sangwish pointed out faint depressions in the grass. He said three people had been lying near the fire and showed where one had been pulled away towards the railway ties. He was sure the marks were made by men.

"If it had been a dog or an animal that was lying there, I would know the difference," he said.

Sangwish pointed out how, in some spots, the earth was black and the grass was white, the same way it would be for 10 to 20 days after killing a buffalo and spilling its blood into the ground.

Examining the grass around the fire, Sangwish concluded that the three people had lain together for at least half the night and that the person had been killed early in the morning.

"I don't know anything of the clock," Sangwish said, "but I know when midnight is."

With nothing else to do, unemployed labourer Augustus Moore went to the scene one day to look around. The body had been cleared away, but there were still pieces of bone that had been left behind. In a nearby pond, Moore found pieces of the scissors grinder's strange sharpening machine. Moore piled them on the bank and went to Grenfell to tell the police.

Two musicians, Antonio Luciano and Antonio d'Egidio, were at the Royal Hotel in Winnipeg on June 26 when a police officer approached them.

"A person you have been walking with was found murdered," the detective said.

"Who is that?" Luciano asked. "The scissors grinder?"

* * *

Both Antonio Luciano and Antonio d'Egidio had come to Canada from Italy in search of opportunity in the new world, leaving their wives and families in the old country.

D'Egidio landed in New York around Easter of 1893, and ran into Luciano not long after. The men knew each other from childhood in Italy and decided to travel together as they explored the new country.

For months they slept in boxcars and in ditches, going house to house, town to town, playing songs for a dime or a quarter, sometimes for a meal and a night indoors. It was near Washington that the two first crossed paths with Giovanni Peterella, a scissors grinder who was travelling alone.

Peterella was stout, with a heavy growth of beard and a short moustache. His face was fleshy, his features plain. "A solid chunk of a man," one woman remembered later, after his body was found.

Luciano and d'Egidio met the scissors grinder again in Vancouver, then in the mountains near Calgary. They saw him three times between Calgary and Regina early in the summer of 1893.

Luciano and d'Egidio told the police they weren't really friends with the scissors grinder, but would say hello to him, just as they would anybody else.

"We were friendly with everyone on the road," Luciano said.

They recalled seeing the scissors grinder in Saskatchewan, but said they'd quickly parted ways and hadn't given him any more thought until they were arrested for his murder.

"It never occurred to me that there was any occasion to feel troubled...," Luciano said. "It never occurred to me that there was any reason why I should look after the scissors grinder."

At the police station, the musicians played a little music for the officers before being put into a cell.

* * *

Luciano and d'Egidio went to trial early in 1894. The judge would later describe the evidence against them as entirely circumstantial, "but very voluminous."

Numerous people had seen the three men together in the days before the scissors grinder's death, and the men were known sometimes to travel together. The musicians had $300 when they were arrested, and the scissors grinder had earlier been seen with a large wad of cash that was conspicuously missing from his body.

George Dickson had seen the musicians and scissors grinder sitting together beside a bonfire outside Grenfell, at the approximate spot where the body was later found.

When he saw the musicians the day after the fire, they were alone. Dickson had even asked about the scissors grinder, but the musicians said they didn't know anything about him.

"He doesn't belong to us," the men told Dickson.

CPR merchant James Hawkes recalled the scissors grinder's distinctive hat, a drab old thing with two big holes.

When he was arrested in Winnipeg, d'Egidio was wearing a hat with two holes in it.

"I would not swear that there is not another hat in the world with holes in it like that," Hawkes said. But, he added, it was not common for people to wear hats with holes.

The musicians were convicted of murder on February 10, 1894, and sentenced to death.

* * *

As Antonio Luciano and Antonio d'Egidio awaited their executions, friends and acquaintances in New York penned a petition to the Canadian government, asserting that the men had been wrongly convicted and begging for their lives to be spared.

"In the name of justice we earnestly beg that before extinguishing two lives your Excellency should be convinced that the convicted men are guilty," the petition read. "We have no doubt that after mature consideration you will discover that a grave error was made by the jurors of Grenfell court."

The petition said the musicians were known to be hardworking, thrifty, and economical, and that "no surprise should be caused" by the $300 found in their possession.

An ocean away, even the queen of Italy learned of the case. She was poised to discuss it with Queen Victoria, but decided otherwise when an ambassador advised her against it.

From their prison cells in Saskatchewan, both men maintained their innocence and pleaded for mercy as their execution date approached.

"I find myself facing this death without knowing how the thing happened," wrote d'Egidio, in a statement translated from Italian. "From the day I rested on my mother's bosom, I have not been accused of anything in my life. It seems like an illusion which can't be true, a man accused of human blood."

Luciano also prayed for his life, but seemed resigned to his death.

"I hope you will grant my prayers, and if not, I wish you a happy life in this world. I bid you adieu…," he wrote. "Adieu world. … It is no great loss to leave it."

A few days before the execution, Luciano called a jail guard to his cell and confessed to murdering the scissors grinder. He said he alone was responsible for the crime. The confession saved the life of his friend, d'Egidio, who was granted a stay of execution.

Luciano faced the noose alone on May 9, 1894.

As he stood on the scaffold, Luciano retracted his confession and once again proclaimed his innocence, saying he had only confessed to save the life of his friend.

"I die innocent like Jesus Christ. He died for everybody. I die for my partner, d'Egidio," Luciano said. "I made the confession so that both might not die. We are both innocent. I am a stranger in a strange country. No one believes me but Jesus …

"Good-bye, I no kill the man."

In 1901, after nine years in prison, Antonio d'Egidio wrote a letter pleading for his release from prison.

"Before God, I swear that I am perfectly innocent of this great crime or any knowledge of the crime, and do not know why I have to remain in prison the reminder of my life…," he wrote. "I have already spent nine years in penitentiary simply because of my being a stranger in a strange land."

D'Egidio was released from prison on April 22, 1902, at the age of 42, with an understanding he would leave the country immediately.

THE IDEA MAN

*H*e called himself an idea man. Where others saw obstacles, Bob Courvoisier dreamed of potential. Perhaps it was in his blood. If the Courvoisier name sounded familiar, it was because he was a descendent of the famous French creators of Courvoisier cognac.

At least that's what Bob told people.

He told his new friends a lot of things, like how he and Robert Goulet had the same vocal coach, and how his stepfather was actor Sebastian Cabot, and how Courvoisier, a lawyer, stood to inherit a $40-million family fortune. The personable, bright, charismatic Courvoisier, with his wavy dark hair and trim moustache, was the rainmaker of his times, suddenly showing up in town one day in May 1980 and infusing people with excitement for his ideas.

Like the plan to buy Grouse Mountain ski resort in Vancouver, put a dome over it, and create a theme park called Magic Kingdom. Or the one that would see blimps carrying moisture-retaining diatomaceous earth to the Middle East to turn deserts into farmland. And then there was Courvoisier's idea to build Canadian sand cars—modified snowmobiles—that could navigate desert terrain. He was also noodling plans for mini-submarines and a condo project in Maui.

Closer to his home base, in Saskatoon, the idea that seemed to have the most potential was a uranium refinery. At a news conference at a downtown hotel in the fall of 1980, the smooth, persuasive Courvoisier unveiled his plans to the media—as the representative of 20 businessmen who had bought options on tracts of land in hopes of enticing Eldorado Nuclear Limited to the Langham area. He told reporters the investor group was prepared to turn over the options to Eldorado for the right price, setting off a firestorm between pro- and anti-nuclear forces. (But Eldorado's people didn't seem to know anything about it. And Courvoisier's holding company had paid only a dollar deposit for each land option. And the investors at that point actually numbered one.)

But the idea man didn't stop there. After being hired to manage a Saskatoon furniture store, Courvoisier thought bigger, feeling it was time for the city to have its own furniture manufacturing plant. The furniture store owner was so impressed that he became Courvoisier's largest investor and staunchest supporter. "You're far too smart for me," the businessman once told Courvoisier.

Drawing figures on a napkin, Courvoisier showed one man how his $50,000 investment could easily turn into $600,000. Taking out a loan, the man ponied up $55,000. In hindsight, he would later say, "I was led as an ass with a carrot in front of my nose. If my interest waned, the carrot was moved closer."

Fourteen people bought into Courvoisier's grand visions. The investors included students, teachers, farmers, retirees, and even an army engineer. They gave the idea man anywhere from $4,000 to $55,000, for a total of $164,500. With promises of doubling their money in six months, some took out loans or drained savings accounts to get in on the ground floor.

Soon Courvoisier was heading up several companies and a staff of 20 employees. He once hired two private airplanes to take his employees on a trip to Disneyland so they would be inspired when approaching Arab investors to back the Grouse Mountain theme park.

He also had a business trip planned to the Middle East to pick up more than a million dollars from offshore financiers. Courvoisier planned to take several staff members, including his newly married research assistant. Her boss had suggested it might make a nice honeymoon trip. But the last time she saw him was at her wedding, ten days before the trip was to take flight.

The investors had been getting regular newsletters, marked "Confidential to the Partnership," updating them on the growth of their money. When it was time for their healthy dividend cheques to be distributed, a supper meeting was arranged at a restaurant so they and their families could celebrate. Nearly 40 people gathered.

But their rainmaker never showed up that spring night in June 1981. Nor did their cheques.

When the police finally found him seven months later, Courvoisier was Patrick Lane, the well-liked dorm supervisor at Cambridge International College, a Toronto private school. Many of the students went to the airport to see their favourite supervisor taken away in handcuffs by the RCMP.

When he appeared in a Saskatoon courtroom, the man formerly known as Bob Courvoisier, Patrick Lane, Clifford David, Peter Marshall, and Stanley Spack was Clifford David William Maltby. It was a name he didn't use for business because he'd once run into trouble moving "certain property" across state lines, landing him in Leavenworth prison in Kansas for two years. "Maltby" had a bit of trouble travelling to the United States.

At his trial, Maltby stepped into the witness box to defend himself. Regarding the Courvoisier cognac family, Maltby insisted he was from the Courvoisier family, just not that one. He'd actually been raised in foster homes in the Victoria area and had his first brush with the law at 15 when he ran away. He was indeed taught by Robert Goulet's vocal coach, Maltby insisted, and he never said he was related to Sebastian Cabot, just that he was friendly with a man who was the actor's godson.

As for all his dreams, Maltby believed they had potential. The heavy-set, bearded man stood at a blackboard at the front of the courtroom to sketch out his plans, like a professor before his students.

Maltby said he realized his schemes were chewing up more money than they were spitting out. But the idea man saw opportunity, not defeat. Knowing he couldn't deliver the promised dividends, Maltby came up with a plan to borrow the money from the Mafia. In return, his company would launder dirty money for the Mob. The elaborate Middle East trip to meet with investors was merely a front to explain the cash payments. That was the plan anyway, Maltby told the jury, until one of his partners got cold feet.

"My primary talents are in conception and negotiation," he said.

Defence lawyer Morris Bodnar argued that schemes like the theme park and the blimps were just red herrings by the prosecution, since no money had actually been put into them. Putting a rock in a box and selling it must have seemed a crazy idea too once, he added. He insisted his client had been upfront that these were risky investments.

But prosecutor Jeremy Nightingale said they were non-existent investments held out like "carrots" to keep investors interested. He argued Maltby, the man of many names, had simply burned through the money, living a life of luxury in hotels and hiring private planes for "business trips."

The jury returned its verdict: Guilty.

Justice David Wright had his own ideas about Maltby. "He is, in my view, a man possessed of intelligence, ingenuity and a devious turn of mind," the judge told the courtroom. "He is an astute student of human nature and a skillful manipulator of other people's weaknesses, hopes and ambitions. He has lived by his wits in a style that few people could ever afford.

"Confidence men have often been glamorized in fiction and in real life," Wright continued. "That folklore, plus the longstanding idea that white collar crime is somehow less reprehensible than other types of crime has led, I fear, to sentences that are too often lenient." Calling Maltby unscrupulous and a threat to society, the judge sentenced him to five years and six months in prison.

Maltby believed Wright had read him all wrong. He promptly appealed and sought bail.

"I would never attempt to interfere with the course of justice," he wrote in a letter to the court. "I have never before been charged with a crime like this and would certainly never do anything else that would place me in this predicament. I would obey all laws, keep to myself, and live a very quiet existence." It was signed, "Thank you, Clifford Maltby."

Maltby didn't get bail, but he did get a small break on his sentence, a six-month reduction. He might have lived that "very quiet existence" he had once espoused.

But he didn't.

On April Fool's Day 1986, 16 days after his early release from Kingston Penitentiary, Maltby dressed himself like a priest, with a white collar and crucifix. His first choice for a hostage was Liberal leader John Turner, but Maltby grew tired of waiting for him to make an appearance on a downtown Ottawa street. He scouted out the diplomatic offices of Ecuador, Barbados, and Jamaica, but settled for the Bahamian High Commission after noticing the security seemed lax.

Reverend David Clark strode into the downtown office around 4:30 that afternoon, telling staff he had a highly confidential letter to deliver. Vice-consul Janet Rahming accompanied him to the airport, ostensibly to retrieve the letter, which the reverend said he had accidentally left in his other briefcase in a locker. He went inside as she waited with her driver, then the convincing cleric asked for a ride back downtown. The reverend was supposed to be calling a fellow priest when he appeared at Rahming's office to tell her she was being taken hostage. She thought it was a joke—until Clark a.k.a. Maltby pulled out a small handgun. (Later, police would learn the starter pistol had been altered to fire .22-calibre bullets, but would have blown up had anyone pulled the trigger.) Maltby also carried a knife and a container that he claimed held explosive chemicals.

As the hostage-taking stretched into the early morning, Maltby was granted a makeshift news conference at daybreak.

Leaning out the third-floor window, the hostage-taker—a cross dangling on his chest, his dark shirt unbuttoned and blowing in the wind—read a statement to the reporters below. Maltby, who had gone to prison for living on pilfered riches back in Saskatoon, was there now in Ottawa to speak for the homeless.

"What this has all been about primarily are kids who have nothing, who have no opportunity," he said. "They're me when they grow up."

He demanded an Ottawa firehall be turned into a shelter. He also wanted a friend released from the Kingston prison. He and Maltby were to be flown by helicopter to the northern wilderness.

The Bahamian diplomat had realized about 90 minutes into her predicament that Maltby meant her no harm, but he expected to die that day. It was nearly seven o'clock in the morning when Maltby last appeared in the window. The 39-year-old took a drag on his cigarette and peered out at the police, reporters, and onlookers gathered on Kent Street below. From the office building across the street, the gun barrels of sharpshooters were pointed in his direction.

It was over 15 minutes later.

Maltby handed his captive the crucifix he had worn as part of his disguise. "Take this as a souvenir," he told Rahming. "You are a really nice lady.

"Janet," he said, "God bless you."

"God bless you, David," she replied. "And I hope all goes well for you here." Then she walked out of the door. Her captivity was over after 15 hours; Maltby's was just beginning.

His penalty this time was an eight-year prison term.

Rahming would subsequently tell the *Ottawa Citizen* she never once felt threatened by Maltby. "I didn't sense he was a murderer."

But somewhere, somehow, Maltby's dreams turned to nightmares.

He wasn't even out of prison two months when Maltby and a fellow parolee went on a crime spree in Ontario. They found themselves one night in a bar in Stratford, where they asked about a place to stay. Someone mentioned that Douglas Grass, a props maker for the Stratford Shakespeare Festival, was known to take in boarders. He was also gay, the bar patron told Maltby.

Grass was to play the role of King Brannick, king of the underworld, in an upcoming production of *The Maltese Hamlet*. When he left rehearsals that night, he told a friend he was to meet someone who had inquired about his ad for a boarder.

Co-workers went to Grass's house to check on him when he failed to turn up at work the next day. He was dead at age 40, killed by 15 blows from a hammer.

It had been wielded by Maltby. He had never met Grass before, but Maltby concocted a plan to kill the gay rights activist. Maltby had an idea that the slaying would somehow avenge abuse suffered in his youth.

At his sentencing for first-degree murder, the articulate Maltby tried to sell the judge on another notion. He asked for death instead of life. The judge was legally unable to oblige.

"The death penalty, for the thinking man," Maltby told a reporter, "is a godsend."

A DIFFERENT CAT

The two American hunters stand chatting with the store owner.

"This is our first trip up to Saskatchewan," says John. "We called up to Regina, and we wanted to hunt down in the southwestern corner. And I didn't know very much about it, asked about a guide, and they named several and Terry was one of them. He knows the country," the hunter continues.

"Terry's got a different kind of lifestyle," he adds almost as an afterthought.

"He still got his girlfriend with him?" asks the store owner.

"No," replies John. "They broke up, he said. But he had another gal that was …"

His fellow hunter, Tom, finishes the sentence, "one was s'posed to move back in last night though."

The store owner recalls that Terry had a girl up in Winnipeg—"off and on for the last two or three years."

"Yeah, he mentioned her," says John.

"Yeah," the store owner notes, picking up on John's earlier observation. "He's a different cat."

* * *

Terry Murphy knew his way around a stick of dynamite. It was an expertise that came in handy in a rural area. Like when a landowner or the rural municipality needed a hand getting rid of a beaver dam blocking a waterway, Murphy's skill was occasionally called upon.

The explosion rocked the single-storey house shortly before noon on November 14, 1985. But what shook some people even more was when Terry's decapitated body was discovered in the ruins. Two days earlier, Terry had leased a 1985 Buick from Tilden Rent-a-Car in Swift Current. The car, left parked in a yard across the alley at the rear of Murphy's property, had avoided the blast.

But it hadn't escaped completely unscathed. After the explosion, when RCMP officers were digging through what remained of Terry's house and property, they discovered a hole in the trunk lid of the rented Buick. It was the result of a shot-gun fired at close range from outside the vehicle. How it got there was a mystery. A clip of rifle cartridges also lay on the front seat, and a number of shotgun shells littered the floor.

Between the time Terry had picked up the car in Swift Current and the police found it near his house in Neville, about 50 kilometres to the south, the Buick had gained some three hundred kilometres.

The same day—a Tuesday—that Terry had rented the car, he had people over to his house in the evening for a party that stretched into the next day. Terry, who was drinking pretty heavily, had a lot on his mind, not the least of which was his upcoming court case.

The avid hunter was facing 15 charges, mostly under the Saskatchewan Wildlife Act, as well as a couple of criminal gun charges. Terry and two others had been caught in an undercover sting operation, a joint endeavour between conservation officers on both sides of the border, targeting illegal hunting in southwest Saskatchewan. In October that year, two American hunters he knew as Tom and John had hired him to act as a guide for deer hunting. As he would find out later, they were actually officers with the United States Fish and Wildlife Service.

Terry was served a couple of weeks before the gathering at his house with charges that accused him of offences ranging

Exploded house in Neville, 1985. Photographer: Bob Jamieson, courtesy Regina *Leader-Post*.

Shotgun damage to rental car, 1985. Photographer: Bob Jamieson, courtesy Regina *Leader-Post*.

Susan Dawson. Courtesy of the RCMP.

from trafficking in wildlife to careless use of a firearm. Jail was a possibility, his lawyer warned him.

Those charges, due soon to come up in court, weren't sitting well with Terry. As some of the party-goers left his house on Wednesday, Terry shook their hands and said he would not be seeing them again. He had a plan to get even with the conservation officers who had targeted him, he told them. That plan involved wiring up a vehicle with explosives and luring the conservation officers to it.

Then he would set off the explosives, killing the officers as well as himself.

A friend stopped by Terry's house later that day but found no one home. Not even the dogs, who normally barked at visitors, could be seen or heard. But the rental car was still parked at the house.

The next day came the blast that ripped apart Terry and his house. The RCMP investigators who sifted through the debris knew it was caused by a bundle of dynamite, perhaps as many as 10 sticks. But what they could not sort out was whether it had been an accidental or intentional act.

And something else was strangely absent.

About three weeks before the explosion, Susan Lynn Dawson, a 27-year-old woman originally from Winnipeg, had moved into Terry's house. A loner who liked to spend time outdoors, Susan had a passion for camping in peaceful solitude near the coulees in the area. Her constant companion was her dog, a blue heeler.

She usually called her family in Winnipeg every couple of weeks. They heard from her last on a Monday. It was

November 10, 1985. She was in good spirits, and nothing she said caused anyone concern. She was among those at Terry's party two days later.

There was no reason to believe she had any plans to move away.

Her yellow truck was found in town after the explosion. It was parked outside an old store owned by Terry. But what police officers didn't find was her purse or some of her missing clothing.

And they never found Susan or her dog.

RCMP investigators suspect Susan Dawson met with foul play after the party at Terry Murphy's residence. But they haven't found any trace of her, not in the rubble of the explosion or anywhere else.

OLD BLUE EYES

I t's like that moment of high drama in the O. J. Simpson case, when he pulls on the glove left at the crime scene—and it doesn't fit.

Except, this is in a courtroom in Regina, Saskatchewan, not the southern United States. The judge is Malone, not Ito. And the accused is on trial for bank robbery, not murder.

A woman steps out of the witness box, walks across the courtroom, and looks intently at John A. McPherson. He stares back at her from his seat in the prisoner's box. Twenty-four eyes—those of the jurors—are darting between the witness and the accused. Defence lawyer Bruce Campbell has just asked a question that could seal McPherson's fate.

Are those the eyes of the robber?

* * *

The attention of most of the traumatized staff that day was focused on the gun.

It was the Friday before the Thanksgiving long weekend when the two bandits walked into the Earl Grey Credit Union around two o'clock in the afternoon. Each had a black balaclava covering his face. The taller, well-built one took control. He was calm and cool, and he had a gun in his hands—hands that were covered by surgical gloves.

"This is a holdup," he said, adding, "This is no joke."

While the smaller guy emptied the cash drawers, the gunman pointed to the vault, and the four employees and one customer got inside. Then the gunman, a big man almost six feet tall, shut the door.

When the robbers stepped out of the bank onto the village's Main Street, they had $25,097 of mostly $20 bills in a small, grey bag. The men left in a black car. Ten minutes later, the five people locked in the vault managed to get out and get help.

The next month, in November 1997, McPherson was arrested.

Investigators thought they had built a strong case. They had even clinched it with two key witnesses—a teen who said he had joined McPherson, the gunman, inside the bank, and another man who said he drove the getaway car. They told a courtroom how they divvied up some of the cash, then buried the rest in a grey bag, with the gun and disguises, in postholes on a farm. And police did find McPherson's fingerprint on a plastic bag containing surgical gloves. A mud-stained grey bag, like the one used in the robbery, was found at McPherson's house.

What they didn't find was most of the money, including roughly $1,200 the teen said he had tossed away into dumpsters because he felt so guilty.

There were some suspicious-looking purchases McPherson had made, like spending $4,000 on his girlfriend a week after the robbery. The money bought a $500 luxury stay at the Hotel Saskatchewan in downtown Regina, as well as a van, paid for with 175 $20 bills.

The robber, the one with the gun, left an indelible impression on several of the witnesses. They remembered his cold blue eyes and blond hair.

But when the loans officer peers into McPherson's eyes from the witness stand, they don't fit—not with her description of the robber, not with the ones given by some of the other bank employees. They were quite certain the robber had blue eyes.

McPherson stares back—with brown eyes.

"They weren't the eyes you saw, were they?" asks Campbell.

"No," she replies.

There is also something else. The dark-haired McPherson has ugly looking scars marring his lower arms. And yet none of the witnesses remembers them. And the bank employee was certain the hair she saw on the robber's arms, poking out from his mid-length sleeves, was blond. Later, at the request of the jury, McPherson, dragging his leg shackles across the carpeted courtroom floor, shuffles over to the jury box and presents his arms for the 12 men and women to survey the scars and brown hair.

Thirty-five minutes after the robbers left the Earl Grey Credit Union, McPherson walked into the Canada Trust bank in Regina, 65 kilometres away, and made a deposit.

Scars, blond hair, and blue eyes aside, Campbell contends the time doesn't fit either—there is no way McPherson could pull a robbery, bury the evidence, and enter the Regina bank at precisely 2:45 p.m. "There's no way he did it," he says.

The argument has echoes of Johnnie Cochrane's "If it doesn't fit, you must acquit."

Except a police officer covered that distance—from the credit union, to the farm where the clothes and cash were supposedly buried, and on to the Regina bank—in 32 minutes.

"It all fits," Crown prosecutor Jeff Kalmakoff tells the jury. "What it fits into is someone setting up an alibi."

The jurors take nearly six hours over two days to chew on the evidence, or perhaps lack of it. Their verdict is not guilty.

From the prisoner's box, McPherson immediately gestures to his girlfriend, forming his fingers into a ring being put on a finger, and she nods back, accepting his proposal. His brown eyes light up with a broad smile as he kneels so a guard can unlock the leg shackles. McPherson spent six months in custody waiting for this day. The 36-year-old acquitted man shakes hands with Campbell, and leaves the court one satisfied customer of the justice system.

* * *

It was like that moment of high drama in the O. J. Simpson case, when police officers chased the prime suspect down a us highway.

Except this was a silver Volvo, not a white Bronco. And it was in Gainesville, Florida, not Los Angeles, California. And this was a high-speed chase, not a slow pursuit.

As the car raced down Interstate 75 at more than 100 miles an hour, weaving in and out between the other vehicles, cash started flying from the windows. Police officers felt confident it was the same money stolen minutes earlier that day, on November 16, 2004, from the First National Bank of Alachua by two masked men. They had been spotted doffing their disguises and climbing into the car.

The tossed cold cash was intended to confound the hot pursuit, as other motorists on the highway stopped and scrambled to pick up the windfall.

When a police helicopter dipped down in front of the getaway car, it veered off onto an exit ramp and slowed, and out ran the passenger, before the fleeing Volvo eventually pulled over on a side road.

From out of the sunroof emerged the driver's hands, stuck up in surrender.

John A. McPherson was behind the wheel.

He had covered the distance from the bank robbery to his arrest in 35 minutes.

*McPherson, if that's really his name, had claimed after his arrest for the Earl Grey robbery that he had once been in the witness protection program. Charged in the Florida robbery and a suspect in several more, he would never again stand trial. The man known as John A. McPherson took his life in a Florida prison.

WRONG TURN

The Thunderbird had once been a bright red and white, but it was nearly unrecognizable after the fire. When the Mounties arrived, the remnants of the car and the scorched grass around it told a seemingly simple tale. The car had become stuck near a slough and overheated when the frustrated but determined driver tried several times to manoeuvre it out of the mud. The overheated manifold had ignited the grass, and the fire had likely spread to the gasoline tank.

Whoever might have been driving had apparently walked away with the keys, abandoning the car in the bush on the White Bear First Nation. It was in an isolated wooded area, almost two kilometres off the main highway. The car had not been reported missing, nor had any of its occupants.

Case closed.

That was October 30, 1985.

It was April the next year when hunters found the keys to the T-Bird. They were near a beaver dam—more than a kilometre from where the car had caught fire. And that wasn't all they discovered. There were also a woman's coat, a cowboy boot with a stylish spiked heel, and pieces of children's clothing scattered in the bush.

Investigators went back to the area where the burned-out car had been spotted six months earlier. They found a suitcase, hidden almost a hundred metres away in the bush. It

The Molinas' burned vehicle. Courtesy of the RCMP.

appeared untouched, still packed with clothes, a camera, a baby bottle, and a passport. There were also three garbage bags filled with clothing, which, like the suitcase, had been removed from the car before the fire and stashed in the trees. The slough was drained that June in an effort to locate the car's missing occupants—to no avail.

Now police had a mystery.

* * *

In Maria's mind, the voices were loud, the messages sometimes garbled, or so clear they were unsettling. They left the Winnipeg woman feeling uncertain and frightened. Alone.

Except, Maria wasn't alone. She had her children, her two smiling, little dark-haired boys who needed her. But that need was sometimes one more thing that overwhelmed the woman challenged by mental illness. Psychotic episodes, which seemed to overtake her suddenly at times, left her seeing and hearing things that were all too real, if only to her.

Maria also had struggles that exceeded those waged in her fragile mind. Unable to keep up with the bills, Maria and her boys had been evicted from their Winnipeg home by the fall of 1985. Her massage parlour, 69 Studio, which had attracted a $300 fine almost a year earlier on a charge of keeping a common bawdy house, was in financial ruin. Maria's Thunderbird had also been repossessed, but she found a way to get it back with a spare set of keys. The family moved in temporarily with a friend, but within a few days Maria had plans to move, maybe to Toronto, where she had lived when she first came to Canada from Colombia back in 1975, or perhaps to Vancouver.

Maria called her estranged common-law husband in late October and asked him to meet her at the bus depot. He arrived to find a dishevelled, lost, and confused woman. Jonathan had no shoes, and Benjamin, the baby, smelled as if he was badly in need of a change, and had been for some time.

Around two o'clock in the morning, they went to St. Boniface Hospital. Maria was no stranger to psychiatric treatment. Ralph Larry, the father of Benjamin and Jonathan, would later tell a *Winnipeg Free Press* reporter that although a doctor believed Maria was in need of mental help, he didn't have the power to hold her against her will.

When Larry last spoke to his wife by phone, on October 28, 1985, Maria promised to call him right back.

She never did.

Maria pulled the Thunderbird to a stop in a farmyard near Langbank, in southeast Saskatchewan. Three-year-old Jonathan headed for the house, pushing open the door without knocking as if he'd lived there all his life. Maria followed, carrying 11-month-old Benjamin. Making herself equally at home, Maria went to use the washroom while Jonathan checked out the kitchen. Moments later, when the mother and her sons pulled out of the yard, it was with milk and fruit—shared by the homeowners. They had never met the Molinas before the trio walked into their home that morning around eleven o'clock on October 29, 1985.

When she left the farmhouse, Maria nearly forgot her eldest son until reminded about him by the farmer. She asked for directions to Vancouver. But at the end of the farm road,

Maria made a right turn instead of the left needed to take her to the Trans-Canada Highway. Her odd behaviour prompted the farm couple to put in a call to the RCMP.

The road Maria took carried her to Carlyle, not the coast. In the small town, she found her way to the Moose Mountain Pontiac service station. An attendant fuelled up the Thunderbird and fixed a tire on the car. It was shortly after 4:30 in the afternoon, and the bus to Winnipeg had also recently pulled into the station. Maria, who seemed confused, asked about the cost of a bus ticket to Vancouver—only to learn it was much more than the $13 dollars she carried. She asked next about a ticket to Regina. By the time the bus pulled out of the station, the T-Bird was gone. Two hours later, a resident of the White Bear First Nation spotted the smoke from the burning vehicle.

* * *

Nearly a year after Maria had steered her Thunderbird north from Carlyle, taken a side road off Highway 9, and followed a trail into the forest dotted by sloughs on the White Bear First Nation, police learned where that path had led. An extensive grid search on October 1, 1986, of the area around where the burned-out shell of the Thunderbird had been discovered turned up the skeletal remains of 39-year-old Maria and her youngest son, Benjamin Michael Molina. They were close to each other, but nowhere near the abandoned vehicle—separated by about a kilometre in a diagonal line from the site where the T-Bird had burned, but still some three hundred metres shy of where the car keys were found.

The mother and son had apparently wandered in the bush until dying from exposure to the elements. The temperature never reached above 10 degrees Celsius that evening and slowly fell through the night and next day.

A knit sweater was found wrapped around Benjamin. Someone, likely Maria, had used a diaper pin with a baby blue clasp to attach a fine gold necklace with a broken chain

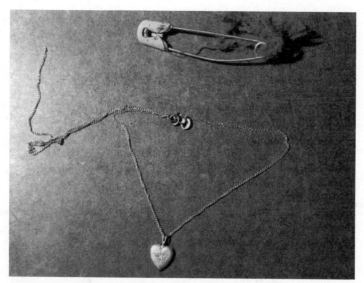

The recovered locket and diaper pin. Courtesy of the RCMP.

to the collar. From it hung a tiny gold locket that could have been so easily lost in the fire, in the woods, or in the chaos of Maria's delusions.

What police never found was one small child, Jonathan Uriah Molina.

FANCY WORK

"**S**orry to be delayed," Mariam said, rushing through the doorway of her friend's High Street home. "But better late than never," she added. It was 9:00 p.m., and the other women had already been there an hour. Mariam Kent was so busy these days, between the Temperance League, the Shakespeare Club, and her work with the church.

Removing her coat and shawl, Mariam picked up her bag of fancy needlework and made her way to a chair, joining the others whose hands were already busy. Her host, Gladys Cochrane, suggested Mariam take a seat closer to the light.

She seemed in good spirits, holding out her handiwork for the other women to see. "I think it will look pretty when it is done," she said.

But her mood went from spirited to distressed about 10 minutes later. "Oh girls, I feel so funny." Mariam was still for a minute, then lifted her hands to her head. "Everything is getting black."

Mariam told the women how she had taken a dose of medicine before coming over—medicine that she believed had come from Mrs. Grayson. Plagued by indigestion lately, Mariam had been using effervescent salt and magnesia. But the home remedies were not bringing much relief. Now, it wasn't only her stomach that was feeling queasy. She regretted having taken even a drop of the medicine.

"I wish I hadn't. I don't feel well at all," she told her friends. Her condition deteriorated rapidly.

Gladys Cochrane ran for a glass of water while the others tried to comfort the woman who was now writhing in agony. "Oh Hazel, Hazel," Mariam called out, grasping her sister's hand.

Hearing the commotion, Gladys's mother came from upstairs and immediately telephoned for Mariam's husband at the store. Gladys followed with a call for Dr. Radcliffe. He wasn't at his house, but the woman who answered promised to get the doctor from his office.

The women helped Mariam—her body wracked by spasms—to the floor and placed a cushion beneath her head. "I am having a fit. I am getting all stiff," she cried. "My God. My God. What is it?" she pleaded. "This is awful."

By the time her husband arrived, she could barely say anything, but grabbed for his hand. "Allie, Allie," she cried out. Taking in the frantic state of his wife, Alexander Kent quickly rushed out the door to find the doctor. The women tried in vain to pour water into Mariam's mouth, but she couldn't swallow. They loosened her clothing and waited for the doctor.

Unconscious and without a pulse, Mariam was beyond Dr. Radcliffe's help when he arrived minutes later. There were a few final gasps, and then her end came. A half hour after her arrival at the Cochrane home on April 3, 1909, May Mariam Kent was dead. The life she had carried in her womb for seven months also ended in death.

The next morning at Zion Methodist Church, where Mariam usually helped with the boys' Sunday school class, even the minister was overcome by grief at such a tragic loss. Ten minutes into his sermon, Reverend E. J. Chegwin found it impossible to continue and brought the service to a close.

The *Moose Jaw Evening Times* called Mrs. Kent "one of the most highly respected ladies in Moose Jaw." In the three and a half years since she had married Alexander J. Kent, of Kent and Brown Men's Furnishings, and moved to Moose Jaw, Mariam had become well-ensconced and well-liked in the community. "She was a power of good among all who knew her," the newspaper article continued. And that made it all the more baffling the next day when further news broke about what had killed the 32-year-old woman.

After leaving the Cochrane house, Dr. Radcliffe went with Mr. Kent back to the couple's High Street home. There they found a one-ounce brown bottle—its paraffin seal broken—next to a teaspoon and a glass. Lifting the unlabelled bottle up to the light, the doctor noticed it still held a small amount of a greenish-blue fluid. Strychnine.

The bottle that had carried the poison ordinarily used to kill gophers had arrived at the Kent home in a parcel delivered by a messenger boy Saturday afternoon. Mariam had passed that afternoon shopping with her sister Hazel Kyle, who resided at the Kent home, and doing needlework.

Later that evening, the phone rang as Mariam, her husband, Mariam's sister Hazel, her sister-in-law Jessie Kent, and Mina Glennie, a stenographer who roomed with the Kents, were finishing supper. Hazel answered and called for Mariam, who seemed to have trouble hearing or understanding the caller. "Mrs. A. K. Grayson?" she repeated. Then, "Mrs. John Grayson?" And finally, "Hazel and I were going out, but I can wait and go later."

After the call, Mariam returned to the dining room and told those gathered that Mrs. Grayson was coming by that evening. She told Hazel to go on ahead to Miss Cochrane's as she would be delayed because of her expected visitor. Mariam wondered aloud about what Mrs. Grayson would have to see her about, given that they were more acquaintances than friends. Indeed, she hadn't even recognized Mrs. Grayson's voice on the phone, she admitted. "That's peculiar," said Mariam. "I did not know Mrs. Grayson has a telephone."

She made no mention of any medicine to those around the supper table.

Mariam asked her husband to put a fire in the furnace before he returned to the store, around 8:00 p.m. "Be sure and bring some fruit home with you tonight," were her last words as he left the house.

Hazel left for the Cochranes' around the same time, while Miss Glennie sat reading a book and Mariam penned a letter to her mother in New Brunswick. She wrote about her dress-fitting that day, how her sister was doing in her exams, the couple's plan to move into a nicer house come the start of May, and how she was feeling better and could eat now without so much distress. Mariam also told her mother how she and Hazel were supposed to go out that evening. "But Mrs. John Grayson phoned. She was coming in, so Hazel will go alone," she said. Mariam started a letter to a friend and again mentioned the plans for the future.

Both letters were still on the writing table after the author's death.

The only visitor before Miss Glennie left the house around 8:30 that evening to attend a concert was Mrs. Cottrell, who had inquired about some work. Mrs. Kent had suggested the woman return at the start of May, a month before the expected arrival of Mariam's child.

Miss Glennie was surprised when she got to the concert and spotted Mrs. Grayson there, since Miss Glennie had understood that Mrs. Grayson was to be Mrs. Kent's visitor that evening. If Mariam met with anyone remains a mystery. She showed up about 30 minutes later at the Cochranes' house and complained of Mrs. Grayson's medicine making her ill.

However, Miss Mary Grayson and her mother, Mrs. John Grayson—Adelia—would later deny that they had made any such call to Mariam or provided her with medicine. They knew Mariam only socially, having seen her last on the Wednesday before her death at the final meeting of the Shakespeare Club, where they listened to a lecture on Mark Twain. They had no reason to send her medicine. Indeed, they didn't even have a telephone in their home. "I am perfectly innocent of all such slander," Mrs. Grayson stated unequivocally during an inquest into Mrs. Kent's death. Mrs. Grayson had a respectable reputation—and someone might have known Mariam would take the medicine if it was given to her in that name, police speculated.

In fact, the call had not come from the Grayson home, but had been made at the train depot pay station. Harriet Hadley, an operator with Moose Jaw telephone central, placed the call to the Kent house shortly after coming on shift at 7:30 p.m. When someone picked up the phone in the Kent house, she advised the caller to drop in the required nickel. The operator heard only pieces of the two-minute conversation—something about a lady feeling sick to her stomach and a boy who couldn't get in leaving something on the doorstep, and the woman at the CPR booth saying something about how to take *it*. Whatever *it* was, "it would help her," the woman told Mariam. The operator thought the caller sounded as if she was laughing.

A fair-haired young woman, described by a CPR security man as having a slight build and a shapely figure, was seen using the phone around that time. She was dressed neatly in a dark skirt—slightly shorter than most women wore as it lifted about three inches off the floor—a fawn-coloured coat, and a dark hat. But who was the woman?

The six-man coroner's jury rejected two theories in Mariam's inexplicable death—that she had deliberately taken her life, or done so accidentally in trying to cause an abortion. According to her husband and her sister, Mariam was excited to be in the "family way." She had miscarried about two years earlier, an event her husband blamed on sheer exhaustion from the Christmas season. "She was pleased. I am positive," her husband told the inquest.

He believed she had been poisoned. "With murderous intent?" Mr. Kent was asked at the inquest. "It looks that way to me," he replied. It appeared that way as well to the coroner's jurors, who concluded Mariam Kent came to her death by strychnine poison "given or sent to her by some party or parties unknown with intent to kill."

Local police and the Royal North-West Mounted Police made little headway in the investigation. At their suggestion, Alexander Kent hired an agent from the Thiel Detective Service Company of Canada. But an undercover operative from Chicago, brought in from the same agency by the police, also worked in secret on the puzzling case. Rumours were rampant—of a jealous woman after Mariam's husband or a botched abortion or perhaps revenge by some of the women of ill repute. Several had been run out of town by a Methodist minister and church members, perhaps Mariam included, in a crusade against the sporting houses that winter.

In updates to the police, the undercover detective reported that he had been frequenting the sporting houses and a men's club as he tried to gather intelligence. "Had several drinks and cigars and played poker for a short time and operative lost $1.00 in the game," said one report.

In another, he said he had met with a number of the girls at four of the houses and bought several drinks at two dollars each. At the City View, he asked a woman named Leone about the church crusade against the houses and was told, "This don't bother us any, and we pay no attention to them. The only time it bothers us any is when we are pinched. And we have to expect this once in a while."

It sure didn't sound like any sort of grudge that might spark murder.

An intriguing anonymous letter was sent to police three months after Mariam's death. "There are a band of ignorant, swindling females over-running the West at the present," it warned. "The old hay fork swindler was only an amateur compared to their methods as they operate on the fears and ignorance of unfortunate and foolish women. They canvas from house to house and have been schooled in all the arts of the swindle by a regular staff of instructors in Toronto … They carry around tons of circulars and some very immoral looking sheets of sexual description. They call their headquarters the Viani Company." The mystery writer suggested several such women were in Moose Jaw plying their "nefarious trade" at the time of Mariam's death. "They carry trunks full of fake remedies and much of it is poison."

Police checked the tip out as best they could, but didn't put much stock in it.

But officers put much more effort into another letter, written three days before Mariam's death. Sent to a Winnipeg drug company by a Mr. A. La Craig of Moose Jaw, the letter said the writer sought "a poisonous powder that would kill an animal instantly." Stamps were enclosed to pay for the powder, to be sent by mail. The writer also sought the price of Hinds Honey and Almond Cream, Pompeian Massage Cream, and Colgate's Toilet Water in a violet scent. The proprietor sent a reply, returning the 10¢, and writing, "We think you had better buy your poisonous powders from some druggist with whom you are acquainted."

Police sent the letter for handwriting analysis, and it was matched to a Moose Jaw woman whose husband had recently died of typhoid. She and Alex Kent had dated on occasion before marrying their spouses, and she still frequented his store.

She did ultimately admit to being the author of the letter. Plagued by depression, the woman said she wanted the poison for herself—but then abandoned her suicidal plan. And—when details about her whereabouts on the day Mariam died checked out—that theory too was rejected.

The coroner offered a reward of $25 for the boy who had delivered the poisonous parcel to the Kent home. But it yielded no results.

Mariam's parents, who had been expected to come for the birth of their grandchild, instead travelled to Moose Jaw to bury their daughter. The organ played softly as the casket was brought into Zion Methodist Church, followed by the dead woman's husband, brother, sister, and parents. Mr. Kent sat with his head bowed through most of the service.

Reverend Chegwin tried to offer comfort with his sermon. "Remember the Psalmist's words," he said. "Yea though I walk through the valley of the shadow of death, I shall fear no evil."

The source of the evil that Mariam had failed even to comprehend when she took her "medicine" was never discovered. Twenty-seven years after his wife's death, Mr. Kent followed. The couple lie next to each other in a Moose Jaw graveyard.

THE SMOKING GUNMAN

He went to war as John Lee. At least, that's the name he used when he enlisted with the Canadian Expeditionary Force on June 9, 1916, in Montreal. He gave his year of birth as 1897, which would have made the young British-born man 19 years old as of his birthday, three days earlier.

He signed his name "Jack Lee."

Private Lee shipped off overseas and spent two years fighting in the First World War before anyone was the wiser. When he was injured in France, someone finally sorted out that the man was really a boy.

He had come to Canada at age 14. And his name wasn't Jack or John or Lee. While he had correctly given his birth-place as London, England, when he enlisted, he was actually born on December 6, 1900. "MINOR" appears in bold letters, all capitals, on a declaration signed by Andrew Vanderberg in August 1918, admitting he had lied about his name and age. Only 15 when he went to war, he was still too young to enlist when he was "demobilized" and sent back to Canada.

* * *

Children peeking through a window were unfortunately the ones to find Gustav Stahl's bloodied and battered corpse. A railway section foreman, he had been on relief duty at Bresaylor, on the line northwest of North Battleford. He lay on a bed inside the section house, although a pool of blood outside the door to his shack suggested that's where he had encountered his killer. Shot through the head, Stahl had also been bludgeoned with a blunt object. His pockets had been rifled; gone were his gold watch and cash.

The best lead was a stranger seen in the area that weekend—a man of about 35 years in age, 185 pounds, wearing a sweater, overalls, and dark peaked cap. Some residents had heard what sounded like shots that Saturday night, on August 6, 1921, but no one looked for the source. The killer could have easily hopped on a train and quickly vanished.

The police thought they had their man when they arrested Jack Masterman, a seemingly suspicious-looking stranger walking along a trail near Lloydminster. He didn't give up without a fight, pulling out a revolver and firing straight at Constable L. A. Hammick, who was joined by Detective Sergeant Robert Scotney of the Saskatchewan Provincial Police. Fortunately the gun misfired the first time, and Masterman's aim wasn't very good the second time around. Scotney managed to overpower the man, who also had a hunting knife, and get him on the ground.

Masterman was no innocent—he had tried to kill the officers, had stolen a police magistrate's car in Lloydminster a day before Stahl's slaying, and had broken into a store in Marshall a year earlier. But, as it turned out, he appeared not to have killed Stahl.

The problem was, it was harvest time and there were a lot of strangers around, hiring themselves out for work on farms. That's how the police ended up talking to Frank Carter, who was working on a farm near Lloydminster. He had plenty to tell the detectives about Walter J. Ferrier. Carter recalled how the man had hightailed it to Edmonton shortly after Stahl had been killed. And he remembered Ferrier making some incriminating statements, like how, when they had talked in a North Battleford poolroom on August 5, Ferrier said he planned to rob Stahl. Later, Ferrier boasted to Carter about killing the railwayman and stealing $322 and a watch.

Ferrier was arrested a few days later in Edmonton and brought back to Saskatchewan to stand trial for Stahl's murder. The star witness at the preliminary hearing was Frank Carter. Based largely on Carter's damning testimony and little else—no smoking gun, stolen money, or pilfered watch—Ferrier was committed to stand trial.

After the preliminary hearing, Carter offered to help police find the stolen goods and the murder weapon. Certain he could arrange a meeting with Ferrier's accomplices, Carter wanted a gun for his own protection, he told police. Scotney obliged, although not completely. He gave Carter an old revolver that was seemingly inoperable.

Not wanting to arouse suspicions among the culprits, Carter insisted that Scotney keep his distance. The hired-harvester-turned-police-agent planned to head to Edmonton to meet with Ferrier's men. Scotney waited in Edmonton, then received word from Carter that he was back in Warman, near Saskatoon. Carter reported that he had the stolen watch, the gun, and a willing witness. Charles Durkin claimed he had seen Ferrier with a wad of money and a gun. But it wasn't very long before police saw through his story. Durkin admitted that Carter had offered him $300 to concoct the tale about Ferrier.

Meanwhile, Carter forced a hotel keeper in Vonda to drive him to Saskatoon, where Carter robbed him of his money at gunpoint. It was close to 3:00 a.m. on September 10 when Scotney and several other police officers converged outside an upper-floor suite at the Victoria Rooming House, near the Barry Hotel on the west side of Saskatoon. The room was registered to P. Seelig of Edmonton, but Scotney had no doubt Seelig was actually Carter when a bullet fired through the door narrowly missed the officers and tore into the woodwork on the upper landing.

"I'd just as soon hang for four as one," he shouted through the closed door, admitting he was Stahl's killer. "If any man opens that door, I've got fifty rounds of ammunition, all good ones that I can use to advantage," Carter added. Two more shots followed.

He held officers at bay for 45 minutes before surrendering. "I'm beat. I'm coming out," said Carter. As Scotney took the gun from Carter's hand, the fugitive asked, "Why didn't you fire when I sent the first shot through the door?"

"My God. I don't want the rope," he added. "I wanted to make a fight to the finish. I didn't expect to get out of this room alive."

Carter alias Seelig was actually former boy solider Andrew Vanderberg. He was spared a noose, but sentenced to life in prison.

* * *

Reginald Eddie Kaye was 16 when he joined the army in May 1937. He got on pretty well with the other soldiers of the 12th Lancers, with the exception of a certain corporal who could be quite unpleasant. Kaye tried to get a transfer, but it was denied. So he and a fellow soldier decided they would walk away.

Andrew Vanderberg had served 16 years of his life sentence when his jailers released him in February 1937. He was deported back to England and, nine months later, joined the army. It was the last day of February 1938 when he and Kaye became deserters.

They did not leave empty-handed. Each took a .38-calibre revolver and plenty of ammunition.

"When I cut loose, you must cut loose," Vanderberg told Kaye.

They pulled out those revolvers when they stole a car from a police officer. The pair got only three miles before the vehicle seized up. A Royal Air Force officer stopped to help two men having car trouble—and ended up being forced at gunpoint to drive them in his vehicle to London, where he left Kaye and Vanderberg in the early morning on March 1. After holding up a shopkeeper, the deserter desperadoes commandeered at gunpoint another car and its driver, who turned out to be a police officer. The quick-thinking Constable Elliott Pillar jammed on the brakes as he neared a police station, and the car skidded into a lamppost.

Swinging round in the car, Pillar grabbed Vanderberg's revolver with one hand and Kaye's gun with the other. One of the car doors swung open, and they all spilled out onto the street. Vanderberg hit Pillar with the butt of the revolver.

"Get back and reach for it," Vanderberg menaced, pointing the gun at the officer.

Hearing the commotion, Sergeant Cecil Rackham ran from the police station as the two gunmen backed down the road.

"Stand back or I fire," the officer heard one of the pair say before they fled.

The officers chased the robbers down Vicarage Lane, over a fence, and into a garden. At one point, Rackham heard someone shout, "Down 'em," followed by a shot.

Rackham flung himself at the teen and wrapped one arm around his neck and head, taking him to the ground. The officer felt a pistol pressing into his left side followed by a sharp sting. He was shot, but still managed to hang on as a fellow constable wrestled the gun from the youth's hand and struck him on the head with the pistol. The shot, entering Rackham's groin area, had passed through his body and narrowly missed his spine as it exited.

Meanwhile, Sergeant George Hemley rushed at Vanderberg. The officer felt a sting in his wrist but still managed to grab hold of the soldier's throat and force his head through a window. At that point, Vanderberg tossed his gun away and gave up.

At the trial, Kaye blamed his actions on his fear of Vanderberg. The teen insisted he never wanted to shoot anyone but was forced to go along by the older man. The judge gave Kaye a break because of his youth. Sentencing him to three years in a detention centre, Justice Asquith told him, "You must consider yourself extremely lucky."

At age 37, Vanderberg could hardly blame his growing list of crimes on youthful folly.

"This is one of the most amazing narratives of sensational crime which this court has heard for a long time," Vanderberg's lawyer, J. C. Llewellyn, conceded. "You may wonder what is the explanation how these crimes ever came to be perpetrated at all," he told the judge, "and how Vanderberg, finding himself in a good position in the army with hopes of promotion, suddenly took to this frightful series of crimes.

"The explanation of his astounding conduct is that he had drugged himself with a drug known as marihuana," Llewellyn said. "It is almost unknown in this country, but is a curse in Mexico and the lower states of America."

Upon making inquiries, the lawyer discovered the drug was smoked, like a cigarette, he told the judge. The effects were "exhilaration, excitement and hallucination."

Llewellyn said Vanderberg had just come off duty when he got some of the drug and smoked it. "It was only after he had got into a state of exhilaration that the question of deserting arose and as he was by that time far from normal, this series of crimes began."

Vanderberg's claim of reefer madness found no favour with the judge that first day of April in 1938.

"The effect on society is exactly the same whether you committed these crimes under the influence of a drug or not," said Justice Asquith.

"It cannot be too clearly understood in this country that the methods of the gangster and the gunman are not going to be tolerated."

He sentenced Vanderberg to 10 years of "penal servitude."

THE INTERVIEW

Impressed with the man's work, the boss has requested a private interview. When Brian arrives, a woman shows him to a side room and quietly closes the door. Alex,* head of an organization with a national and international presence, invites Brian to have a seat.

"John has taken a big leap of faith in you," says Alex, believing it's time for Brian to play a bigger role. But the boss needs to satisfy himself that it's the right move. "Please tell me a bit about yourself."

Brian isn't sure exactly where to start. He mentions his work as a unit chief for an ambulance service, how he had been an assistant chief with a fire department, and superintendent of health safety and security for a mining company. He also had his pilot's licence, Brian says, although he hasn't flown in 21 years.

"What is it that you think I can do for you?" Alex asks after a bit.

Again, Brian stumbles to find the right words. "Uh, provide me with a lifetime opportunity to, uh, be as good as I want to be."

"Anything else?" asks Alex.

"I think that pretty much sums it up," Brian replies. "To be the best that I can be. I pride myself on being very, very aware of what's going on, and doing the job absolutely to the best of my capabilities.

"You asked what you could do for me. You've already done that for me," he continues, between sips of his drink. "You have boosted my belief that I am capable of being of value to somebody. That's what I'm interested in."

Feeling confident he has the right man, Alex asks, "So you foresee a future for yourself here?"

"Yes I do," Brian replies.

As a boss, Alex values dependability, loyalty, and honesty. Before he gives Brian a commitment, he wants a show of those values. Brian has a "situation" that he needs Alex's help with. "I'd like you to tell me as much detail and information as you can," says the boss.

Alex and his outfit already know Brian very well. They should. They've been on his case since 2003. That's the year Scotty Hauser turned up dead in a dumpster in the back of a Vernon, British Columbia, hotel undergoing renovations. Brian lived nearby, and he knew Scotty, who occasionally dropped by Brian's crack house to buy drugs.

When the body of the 42-year-old drug addict was found under some suspicious circumstances that June, the police started questioning Brian. But he didn't have any answers for them.

After a while, the police tried something new. It was October 2003 when Brian made a new friend—an ex-con just like Brian, except one with better connections. He introduced Brian to people who put him to work. Brian was at the hotel room as backup when one guy got roughed up for not paying his debts. And he was there at the border when a cache of explosives was handed over to someone who made mention of potentially blowing up a shopping mall. Brian also helped get rid of things, like evidence. Brian was eager to help. And with each successful job, the man from Lucky Road in Kelowna felt more confident he had a future in this "criminal" organization.

As Brian and the boss sit across from each other on a boat in Vancouver harbour three years after Scotty's death, Alex agrees to help fix Brian's "situation." But first Brian has to do something for him—tell Alex exactly what happened.

Brian talks about the "street beggar" he supplied with crack cocaine. The guy owed Brian $100, and they argued.

"I did take him out. I put him in the dumpster," says Brian, adding that he thought he had been thorough in "cleaning up." But maybe not.

"I think the cops are now knocking on my door," he adds, "because they'd like to put a little bit of pressure on—just to see how I react."

Alex presses for more details, asking what Brian means by "taking him out."

Brian used a crescent wrench, catching his victim right behind the ear. But Brian didn't think he hit hard enough because they ended up in a struggle. Brian says he grabbed his victim by the throat and kept on choking until he stopped moving.

Alex understands. You can't let people like that screw you around. It's business, and then you have some guy who thinks he can take advantage. "Am I correct?" he says.

"That's the way I look at it," Brian agrees. Later he adds, "He was nothin'. He was skin and bones ... No problem at all." Brian explains how he put an oversized pillowcase over the man's feet and slid it up, and pulled another down over the man's head, threw the wrench inside the case, and secured them with plastic ties. Then he left the corpse in the dumpster.

There is just one problem. Alex has seen the autopsy report. He tells Brian the man didn't die from strangulation—so maybe he hasn't told him everything he knows. The pillowcase and the ties were right. But Scotty Hauser died from a drug overdose. He wasn't hit with a wrench; it was likely something more like a fishing gaff, which Brian happened to have inside his house.

Still, Alex and the other Mounties who are part of this sting figure they've heard enough. Brian has pretty much confessed to killing Scotty.

Alex, acting as the boss in the scenario, thought he'd play along a little longer. During one of the "jobs"—also set-ups—Brian had hinted he might know about another crime since he had talked about dumping a gun in Alberta's Bow River. Alex decides to go fishing.

"Let me ask you this, have you ever killed anybody else?" says Alex.

"Yes," Brian replies without hesitation.

This time Alex thinks Brian is lying, trying to make himself look good in front of a man he thinks is the head of some high-level crime mob. "Please do not bullshit me," Alex warns.

Brian says he has no reason to lie. The guy in the dumpster was actually his second kill, he tells Alex. The first happened almost six months earlier. In Saskatoon. Brian was in the city on a business trip, delivering a safety training seminar for a tire company. Brian picked up a woman in the company car he was driving. "She didn't wanna come across," he says, so he raped and strangled her.

Her name was Victoria. "That's all I know," Brian adds.

Alex's mind is racing. Victoria? What the hell is he talking about? The British Columbia Mounties' operation has targeted Brian for the killing of Hauser. The officers have been working the case for almost three years. Those sitting in a nearby hotel room, where they are listening in on the conversation between Brian and Alex, are dumbfounded.

After Brian leaves the meeting, the recording devices that have captured his meeting with the boss also reflect the police officers' surprise at his new revelation. "Think he's lying?" one Mountie asks.

"It's a good lie," another replies.

* * *

Olga Flesjer would always remember the day her first granddaughter was born. It was August 26, 1981, at 3:33 p.m. Olga was waiting outside the delivery room. Minutes later, a nurse brought the newborn out and laid her in her grandmother's eager arms.

"I felt that God had blessed me by sending me an angel." The baby was named Victoria, for Olga's mother.

Years later, Olga would also recall the last time she saw her granddaughter. Victoria, by then living in Saskatoon, had come to Regina to visit her grandmother. They sat and talked long into the evening. The next day, on September 20, 2002, Olga held her granddaughter in her arms and told her "baby" how much she loved her. Then Victoria Jayne Nashacappo left for Saskatoon.

Olga got the phone call a week later saying Victoria was missing.

"Victoria was a gentle girl with hope and dreams every young girl has," her grandmother would tell the court. "It breaks my heart to hear lies spoken about her."

Victoria's dreams included helping children one day. It may have seemed out of reach for someone like Victoria, who'd had her share of troubles, but she was trying. The symbol of those efforts was a green and black backpack. It carried her school books, a black binder filled with paper, some pens, and a purple heart-shaped eraser. Victoria took the backpack to Radius Community Centre for Education, where she was upgrading her high school classes.

When Crystal last saw her sister, Victoria was headed to school. It was Wednesday. Victoria was wearing beige pants and a blue sweater that had been a gift to Crystal from their sister Melissa. Having still not heard from Victoria by Friday, Crystal went to the police.

For years afterwards, Crystal would call out to women who resembled her sister. But when they turned around, they were never Victoria. Their mother, Betty Nashacappo, walked along the riverbank—in hope and dread her daughter's body might appear. Knowing her daughter had left that day with only a sweater, she fretted about her out there in the cold. When Betty could sleep, it was in four-hour stints, out of fear she might miss Victoria's phone call or fail to see her walk past.

Hope faded—but never completely disappeared. A seemingly eternal purgatory of not knowing, and imagining the possibilities, filled the void.

"No one knew nothing," Betty would one day write to the court. "I felt helpless. I felt like nothing can help me now. I no longer felt."

* * *

They stop at Canadian Tire to pick up a shovel and a hatchet, tools for the job. Brian leads his buddies—the ones sent to help take care of this "situation"—to what remains of an old country farmhouse about 20 minutes down the highway south of Saskatoon. When he was there last, in September 2002, the house was still standing. As Brian had suspected would happen even back then, the farmer had since knocked down the crumbling, weather-beaten building.

Brian tells his buddies about how it went down. "I gave her $60 and she says, 'Okay. I'm just a school kid. I want to go home now. Take me home.' And I said, 'No, no. We got a contract sweetie.'" She pleaded again, "Take me home now or I'm going to start screaming."

She never got the chance to say much more, recalls Brian. "I just choked her." He and his friend leave the cleanup expert to the task and head back to Saskatoon.

Back during the meeting, Brian had told Alex that after strangling the young woman he knew only as Victoria, he left her naked body in the root cellar of the old house. He had tossed in her backpack of books and her clothes.

"At what point did she realize she was in trouble?" asked Alex, eager for details that might reveal whether Brian was telling the truth.

"Uhm, probably when I kinda grabbed her and put my arm around her, uh, neck," said Brian. "I think she made a comment like, 'I've always wondered if this would happen.' And then she just sorta went, uh, like, acted as if she passed out. And, uh, and I did my thing, and then uh, and then she got up. Started to walk away and said, 'Can I go now?'"

Brian chuckled as he continued. "I said, 'I don't think so.' And that was when I decided to do what I did.

"Dead people don't talk."

But their killers do. And when what remained of Victoria was pulled from the ruins of the farmhouse three years, nine months, and two days after she was last seen by her sister, the

RCMP officers knew for certain Brian hadn't lied about killing the young woman. A purple scrunchie still held back her dark, shoulder-length hair. Just as Brian had told Alex, her clothing and backpack lay on top of her body.

Betty wanted Brian Robert Casement to hear the truth about her daughter, dead long before she should have been at age 21. "My family's blood was spilled and wasted for nothing," she wrote in a victim-impact statement. "[She was] someone I truly loved and always will and that love you can never have. And you never had her.

"Never."

---

*Pseudonyms have been used for the undercover officers to comply with a court-imposed publication ban. Casement was tried and convicted of first-degree murder in Victoria's death. No one has ever been charged with killing Scotty Hauser.

DAIRY GLASS

Albert Allen's customers remembered him as friendly, even "jovial." The British-born milkman often had a cheery greeting or an affable wave for them. On his street, neighbours admired Allen's well-tended bungalow. But what they remembered most was the way he cared for his children. In the backyard, he had put in a sandpit and swings. And Allen was often seen there playing with his children: Seven-year-old Arthur Robert—Bobby as most called him—was in grade two; next was three-year-old David Albert James; and the only daughter was Glenys Maureen, a busy 16 months old that fall. Strangers and family alike remarked on Allen's affinity for not only his own but also other children in the neighbourhood. He seemed to have so much patience for their games and would be remembered for putting up swings for many children on the block.

"He always had been unusually kind to his children," Allen's father later remarked. "He seemed to enjoy them more than most fathers do."

Allen had worked at Glass Dairies Limited for a couple of years before the tragedy. He had been a baker after leaving school, but switched jobs on the advice of his doctor, who recommended more fresh air. So Allen delivered milk, driving a different route each day to relieve the regular driver.

That September, Allen took a week of sick leave for what was diagnosed as a stomach flu, then asked for more time when he still wasn't feeling well. He was having trouble sleeping and had no appetite, but regularly ate Aspirins to fight his severe headaches. Manager John Glass gave him a week's holiday to rest up. Allen spent some of those days putting a fresh coat of paint on his house.

A steady job, a solid home, a loving wife of eight years, three healthy children – Allen had an idyllic life. But like peering through the curved, thick glass of the milk bottles he picked up and delivered each day, a closer look inside revealed that the outer view was distorted. And just like those glass bottles from the dairy, it was all so very fragile.

* * *

The ladder Allen used when he painted was still propped up outside the front of the house when Sergeant John Wilson and Constable Harold Shires pulled up in a taxi on the morning of September 20, 1946. A can of paint and the brush were nearby. Wilson went around back, put a key into the lock, and opened the door on the four-room bungalow. As he stepped inside the kitchen, the sergeant's gaze fell upon a child's baseball bat lying beside an iron bar in the centre of the floor.

There was blood on the thicker part of the bat, and on the curved end of the bar.

In the southeast bedroom, off the kitchen, the officers found the motionless body of little David on the floor, not far from a homemade bed. His head was slightly turned to the right, as if his brown eyes were looking at something. Or away from someone. His body was still warm, but the blood matting his brown hair and pooling beneath his battered head settled any question of signs of life.

David's sister and playmate lay across the foot of the bed in the second bedroom. As she lay on her left side, Glenys Maureen's right arm was partly beneath her body while her left arm dangled over the side of the bed. Her blood was soaking into the blankets and mattress. Like her brother, she was still warm.

When Mrs. Allen had left after breakfast to do some shopping downtown, her husband had been lying in bed, smoking and staring at the ceiling. She arrived home to see neighbours gathered outside the tidy bungalow as police officers dealt with the mayhem inside.

Bobby had gone to school that morning—fortunately.

The key Wilson used to open the door at 737 18th Street West had landed on his desk that morning. The man who tossed it there was still in his pyjamas and dressing gown, despite his arrival at 11:35 in the morning. However, he had taken the time to pull on a pair of rubber boots and coveralls. He had stepped around the front counter, stopping in front of Wilson.

"Lock me up. I just killed my two kids," Albert James Allen said, tossing a key into a basket.

Wilson helped the pale, shaken man into a chair.

"What did you say?" the officer asked.

Allen repeated: "I have just killed my two kids, and that key is the key to my back door."

A little more than an hour before their father arrived at the police station, Glenys and David had been running around in the house playing. Somehow, they ended up in separate bedrooms. Allen found the baseball bat in his sons' room. Swinging it at his little boy, the father known for his attentiveness to his children connected with his youngest son's head, killing him almost instantly.

Next, Allen walked through the living room into the bedroom where Glenys was and swung the bat again.

His explanation was almost as surprising as his actions that morning. "I loved them all very much," he told the police. "That's why I did it."

Not stopping to wipe his children's blood, which was spilled on his rubber boots, Allen locked the door and went to the police station to tell what he had done. And why.

"I knew I was going crazy, slowly," he said. Allen had been thinking about killing his entire family for some time, planning how best to put them out of their misery.

"It is not that they are in misery now, but I know I am going crazy and they would be in misery later. I loved my wife and children. I do not want them left to suffer that humiliation. I know I did it. I want no leniency. I want to get it over as quick as possible. I want no lawyer or anything like that. I want no mercy. I am not a cold-blooded murderer. I thought they would be better off dead."

And now the justice system would decide if the 27-year-old should also die.

But Allen would not get his wish for swift justice. Judged unfit to stand trial because of insanity, Allen was confined to the Saskatchewan Hospital at North Battleford. Speaking to Allen's wife and parents, psychiatrist Dr. Robert Weil learned Allen had often gone through bouts of melancholy. He was a man of high ideals, and whenever he couldn't meet them, he fell into a dark depression. The doctor found Allen's outlook for his family appeared so bleak that he actually believed death was the better choice. "He might have known for moments that wasn't the normal thing to think, but he couldn't help himself thinking it," Dr. Weil later told a courtroom. Following a diagnosis of manic-depressive psychosis, Allen's treatment included electroshock therapy and water treatments in which he was wrapped in lukewarm sheets while a cold water pack was put on his head for two or three hours at a time. The doctors also tried psychotherapy and group therapy, then a new form of treatment. Slowly Allen improved. He was judged fit enough to be tried for murder almost two years after the crime.

Dr. Weil insisted Allen didn't understand what he was doing when he killed his children. "No normal human being would kill his children without being mentally disturbed," the doctor said.

In less than half an hour—just 28 minutes to be exact—the jury returned with a verdict: Guilty.

Then it was Allen's turn to speak.

Before he could be sentenced to die, Allen stood and spoke, his voice firm as it rose in the hushed courtroom.

"As I stand here before God and before this court and before men, my conscience is clear. I am not guilty of any wilful act as I was charged. I ask any man or woman in this court if they think I wilfully killed my own children. Would any father wilfully kill his own children? I don't think there can be any doubt about that. No father would wilfully kill his own children. The very laws of nature say a father will protect and look after his own children. What is the answer to this? Why did I do these things?

"There is something wrong with me. I have no recollection of my actions. Many things stated in court were as new to me as they were to you." Allen protested the verdict, insisting justice had not been served and pleading for a new trial. Then he tried to make those listening see things as he now clearly saw them.

"My Lord," he said in addressing the judge, "all this tragedy could have been avoided if it were not for the ignorance of my relations and friends. I don't blame them. They didn't know anything about mental illness as I have come to know it since I have seen cases at the hospital, since I became cured. If people had known as I now know myself, this could have been avoided. I went to doctors in this town ... I told him I couldn't sleep, I was doing without sleep. I couldn't sleep. I had periods of black-outs. I have even got lost going home from work. My Lord, he told me to go home and take a rest. I had no knowledge of being sent to Battleford. I had no knowledge I ever had a trial before. These things I swear to Almighty God on any Bible at all and I am not given to lying. Never before in my life have I ever, my Lord, been accused of any crime. Yet today because of the ignorance of people—I say this because I have seen hundreds of men who were mentally ill since I went to the hospital at North Battleford—I am here. If it were not for the ignorance of people, the verdict would not have been guilty this morning."

King's Bench Justice Henry Bigelow was not moved. What he saw was a cold-blooded killer. "It was a cruel, dastardly crime. There was no doubt in my mind, and none in the minds of the jury, that you knew what you had done. You were aware of it, so you weren't entitled to the plea of insanity."

With that, Bigelow sentenced Allen to hang on September 9, 1948.

But Allen would eventually get the mercy he had sought when he made his confession. He won a second trial on appeal. This time, the 12-man jury took 40 minutes and accepted that Allen wasn't driven by murderous intent, but instead by his fragile mental state. The verdict was not guilty by reason of insanity. "That, I admit, is perhaps the only verdict that could be reached on the evidence, and I quite concur," Justice George Taylor said. As Allen left the courtroom to return to the Saskatchewan Hospital, he kissed his relatives and said goodbye.

BEHIND THE EIGHT BALL

They had chosen the location, plotted the route, outfitted the vehicles, relayed the code words, and lined up their people. It was all going to go according to plan—just like the first time. There were a hundred "birds" on the line in that trip. The driver flew to Las Vegas, met the contact in Victorville, California, picked up the cardboard boxes at the shop, and headed northeast for about 2,500 kilometres. Then the boss and his guy met the driver at the border and carried the load back to the west coast.

Emboldened by how smoothly the first run had gone, they arranged the second load less than two months later. The driver went again to the same warehouse for the pickup and tucked the bricks in the hidden compartments in the floor of his truck. But this time, when he met the boss near the border between Montana and Saskatchewan, there was a problem: Snow. Not the illegal sort—the one-kilogram cocaine bricks wrapped in paper and plastic that he'd hauled from California to Canada—but the real deal. The waist-deep white kind delivered by a harsh winter on the prairies.

The trio loaded the bricks of cocaine on a rescue sled—but was tough sledding trying to pull 100 kilograms on a bone-chilling day in February 2010. Not one of these British Columbian boys had envisioned this sort of problem. Running out of options, they buried their "snow" in *the* snow—a multi-million-dollar mound left on the desolate white landscape

Hidden compartment in truck used to haul drugs. Courtesy of the RCMP.

not far from the badlands where outlaws more than a century before made their hideouts.

The next day, the boss—nicknamed "Billy" for Billy the Kid—rode into Moose Jaw and bought a snowmobile. The new sled had no trouble pulling the load to the waiting vehicle. It proved handy for the next three runs.

They didn't hit a snag again until about a month later, on the seventh trip. The driver picked up part of the load in Montebello, California, and more in Hollywood. He took a detour at Redding, where he dropped $12,000 of Billy's cash on a camouflage-coloured Bad Boy Buggy all-terrain vehicle to navigate the spring mud and slush. Another pit stop in Seattle to get the rest of the load, and he headed north, past Plentywood, Montana. The quad helped to cart the bricks across the border to Saskatchewan—and into the hands of Billy and his helper, just like before.

Except this time, the police were on to Billy.

When the Mounties stopped a Ford Fusion on the Trans-Canada Highway near Swift Current, Nugget, an RCMP dog, sniffed out the 151 kilograms of cocaine packed in two large suitcases in the trunk. Troy Ernest Swanson, a 23-year-old laid-off cement truck driver from Vernon, British Columbia, was at the wheel. Next to him was a two-way radio.

Busted.

Scarcely able to believe what was happening, Billy circled past the stopped vehicle twice with his rental car. He pulled into a service station by Swift Current, jumped out and tossed his GPS device and two-way radio into a dumpster, got back in his car, and headed west. The RCMP arrested Billy—a.k.a. Brock Ernest Palfrey—a few days later in British Columbia.

Palfrey and Swanson, who had met and become friends in school, faced their first criminal charges together—importing cocaine and possession for the purpose of trafficking. At that point, the RCMP knew nothing of the 300 kilos of cocaine that had already come across the border on the previous trips or the scale of Palfrey's operation.

He was no street-level dealer. In fact, he wasn't any kind of dealer. More in the business of traffic than trafficking, Palfrey had carved out a niche transporting massive shipments of drugs for whoever wanted to pay, like drug cartels and biker gangs. And his customers didn't take lightly the loss of a load carrying a potential $6.5-million street value. They demanded a money-back guarantee. Palfrey, fearing he might be shot, was determined to make up the losses.

By February 2011, he had found a solution: A new route, new vehicle, new driver, but the same dirty business. This time, Palfrey maximized the trips, sending B.C.-made ecstasy pills south and bringing the cocaine north. Out on $75,000 cash bail, he decided to stay behind the scenes in British Columbia. His key driver in Canada was William Bruce Larsen, a family friend whose skills as a handyman were also put to use building hidden compartments in a pickup truck.

The shipments started flowing again across the border, this time through a secluded, abandoned farmyard in the cattle country south of Val Marie.

"Loaded and gone 147," the US driver texted Palfrey from California in mid-April 2011. The boss obsessively kept in touch with his drivers through encrypted cellphones, known as PGPs for their promise of Pretty Good Privacy.

"Hahaha we run the world," Palfrey subsequently texted in response.

Larsen, making his sixth trip, met the US driver and transferred the bricks into a fake propane tank in the back of his truck.

It was around 3:00 a.m. on April 26 when something tripped a sensor on the border. US officers saw lights in the distance on the Canadian side, and, on the American side near Malta, Montana, found a truck loaded with an all-terrain vehicle. The brake lights on the ATV were disconnected, the instrument panel covered with tape, and the headlights disabled—this Bad Boy didn't want to be seen.

And neither did its driver. That bad boy was questioned by Homeland Security. The young Canadian who had grown accustomed to $700 jeans and $400 shirts as Palfrey's cocaine courier through the States was facing the prospect of years in a Montana prison. The Regina Integrated Drug Unit offered him an alternative.

He was due to make another delivery.

The 35-kilo load was picked up as before. Except it and the US driver were under the control of the police. And this time, Palfrey was none the wiser. Meanwhile, the Mounties, who by then had been reading with interest the driver's encrypted cellphone messages, were quickly getting up to speed on Palfrey's drug network and the players.

"I'm the man, the myth, the legend," Palfrey had once bragged. "Nobody moves more birds than I do," he added, using his code word for the coke.

Except, he was starting to lose more birds. The RCMP intercepted the next two loads—a combined total of 184 kilograms of cocaine—as well as the truck with the hidden compartments.

During one of the pickups, a nervous Larsen had confided to the US driver: "I won't rat you out. I won't rat anybody out. You play the game. You do the time. That's the way the world is ... It's a lot more time if you get caught down there in the States."

After the loss of the two loads, Palfrey scrambled to figure out what was going wrong and his next move. The trusted driver-turned-police-agent met to talk with the boss and Larsen in Vernon—and RCMP officers were listening too.

"So what now?" asked the driver.

"Gotta go to work," replied Larsen. "Billy's a hard man to work for."

The intercepted loads were a setback. "We gotta build another vehicle and gotta get cooking again," Palfrey said. "We'll make more money anyways."

Larsen agreed: "Fifteen trips, and we will be retired."

Confident Larsen could put a new vehicle together in no time, Palfrey said there was another load waiting in Los Angeles. The boss did not want any more of those "weird problems." Talk turned to switching to a family-friendly looking minivan; police seemed to target the half-ton trucks. Maybe they could disguise it with religious stickers, Larsen suggested. He needed about $25,000 to get the van properly outfitted with hidden compartments in the back and under the floor.

"Billy's got to crawl under a rock here in the next year or so," Larsen said at one point. Palfrey mused about Malta— not the city in Montana, but the country in the Mediterranean. "There's no extradition laws there I guess."

* * *

He had a scrap of a map, a corner ripped from southwestern Saskatchewan. It didn't actually reach all the way to the international border, instead stopping around Shaunavon, circled several times over in blue ink. As the time neared 2:30 in the morning, he was hopelessly lost in the dark on back roads, and the needle for the gas was inching towards empty. Worried he was "heated out" and police were on to him, Larsen had lined up a new driver for the minivan. The rookie overshot the

Farmyard near border in southwest Saskatchewan where drug exchanges occurred, 2011. Photographer: Barb Pacholik, courtesy Regina *Leader-Post*.

"drop zone" by half a kilometre—although he didn't actually know he had strayed that far afield. A few hastily exchanged texts with the courier he was supposed to meet from the States eventually got the trainee on track. This wasn't helping the gasoline situation any.

The minivan followed the quad back to the meeting spot. It took mere minutes to swap cargo in the old farmyard. The 35 bricks were packed into the minivan's hidden recesses. And the US driver collected the bags filled with 100,000 BZP pills—akin to the drug ecstasy in a rainbow of blues, pinks, greens, and yellows—and $10,000 cash.

As the minivan headed north, the driver anxiously pulled into a couple of small-town gas stations. Closed. Damn. Back on the Trans-Canada, he spotted the Shell sign at Gull Lake like a beacon in the night—only to find that station also locked up tighter than the border. Running short of options and gas, he parked and waited.

And so did the others—the ones who had him in their sights from Medicine Hat, east along the Trans-Canada Highway into Saskatchewan, through the small towns heading south, all the way to the abandoned farmyard near the Montana-Saskatchewan border. Had he run out of gas before he got to the Shell, the surveillance team had a backup plan, something about a farmer in a pickup truck who happened to keep a can of gas handy. They didn't need it though.

When the station reopened at dawn, he fuelled up and got back to his Medicine Hat hotel room. A few hours later, the rookie driver was on the road again heading west.

He was oblivious to the team on his trail from Saskatchewan, through Alberta, all the way to the foggy, rain-soaked Okanagan Valley in beautiful British Columbia, where the drug officers forced the vehicle to a stop. The new driver had made his first—and last—run for Brock Palfrey.

The boss and Larsen had also reached the end of the road. As a team of officers boxed in the van at an intersection in Salmon Arm that October 1st day in 2011, other teams simultaneously moved in to arrest Larsen, a 51-year-old carpenter-turned-courier residing in a rented farmhouse near Coldstream, as well as Palfrey, who was only 22 years old when he began his illegal international enterprise. Arrested at his cabin backing the Silver Star ski resort near Vernon, the boss had been doing some homework, researching legal cases on how to challenge a search warrant. Swanson, who never moved another load after he was caught near Swift Current, also faced a new raft of charges based on the information gleaned from the PGPs that showed he had made six drug runs.

A year later, all three British Columbian men made return visits to Swift Current for their guilty pleas and sentencings.

It was November 2012 when a young man wearing a tailored black suit, a plum-coloured shirt, polished black leather shoes, and a poppy in his left lapel stepped from an RCMP prisoner van. Brock Palfrey resembled a businessman going to a meeting—except for the shackles around his wrists and ankles.

His family, who had travelled from British Columbia to Swift Current to support him, sat near the front of the

Brock Palfrey, 2012. Photographer: Barb Pacholik, courtesy Regina Leader-Post.

ornate, oak-trimmed, historic courtroom.

Several rows back, blending in like anyone else who may have wandered in to watch the case, sat two of the drug officers who had a hand in the history-making bust, code-named Project Faril. The Roman numerals I, II, III, and IV were added as the investigation moved through the original 151-kilogram seizure along the Trans-Canada in May 2010 to Palfrey's attempts after his arrest in October 2011 to pull together another drug deal while in the remand unit at the Regina Correctional Centre. He tried unsuccessfully to ship two kilos of cocaine to Swift Current—to take care of some debts. The Mounties found out about that deal too, with taps on the cellphone he had smuggled into the jail.

In less than two years, Palfrey and his crew had imported 1,370 kilograms of cocaine and exported 790,000 ecstasy pills in 16 trips—a new high for Saskatchewan. The cocaine alone nearly equalled the weight of a small white rhino, which is what the Americans dubbed the international takedown operation on their side of the border. Police on both sides were left to ponder how many more groups there were like Palfrey's still moving drugs—or the others that would try to fill the gap.

Like several of the officers on the drug squad, one of the two sitting at the back of the courtroom had previously worked in a small northern community. It was the kind of town where the call load escalated when drugs flooded in—

Cocaine packed in a suitcase. Courtesy of the RCMP.

more thefts and break-ins to finance dope deals, more domestic violence, more bar fights, more children who went without food so a desperate addict could buy an eight ball of coke, the standard street-level sale—an eighth of an ounce. At times, the drug-fuelled violence escalated to death.

After his guilty pleas, Palfrey admitted he had never thought about the final destination for the drugs he moved. He gained some insight while on remand with prisoners ranging from petty thieves to killers at the Regina jail. "I now know the effects the products we were transferring have," he told Justice Timothy Keene.

While Palfrey sat in court listening to federal prosecutor Doug Curliss detail the illicit business venture, snow began to fall. It piled up outside the courthouse as the hours passed. Inside, the mounting evidence buried the British Columbian man who had once underestimated snow in Saskatchewan.

Palfrey received an 18-year prison sentence, also a Saskatchewan high; Larsen got 12 years, and Swanson 11 years. At this writing, the Crown had appealed, seeking more time.

NO FIXED ADDRESS

After the arrest, police reported the young man as being of no fixed address. It was true. Valentine Nicholas Leschenko was sort of between residences. Born in Gelk, Belgium, and raised in Ontario, he had plenty of addresses through the years. They were in places like New Westminster, British Columbia; Collins Bay and Kingston, Ontario; Edmonton, Alberta; and Prince Albert, Saskatchewan. He just never really liked to stay anywhere for very long.

So when he caught the bus to Regina in July 1973, Leschenko was only passing through. Police and two bullets changed his plans.

Before rolling into Regina, home for Leschenko had been the penitentiary in New Westminster, where he was serving a 12-year stretch. It had actually started out in November 1972 as nine years for a string of armed robberies in Toronto, but after a prison escape and two more holdups in Vancouver, the sentence grew by three years. Five months after it was imposed, Leschenko and his buddy from the earlier escape left a couple of dummies fashioned from blankets "sleeping" in their cell beds in the New Westminster prison. The real inmates never returned from the recreational grounds. Leschenko and his fellow prisoner holed up in a shed for hours before cutting their way out through the chain-link fences to freedom.

A few days after the July 18, 1973, breakout, Leschenko pulled a break-in at a store in Golden, British Columbia, making off with two revolvers and a rifle. He had one of the pistols and his accomplice had the other when the men—wearing sunglasses, phony beards, and fake moustaches—held up the Toronto-Dominion Bank in downtown Calgary. They left with $3,600, scooped into a plastic bag from the tellers' drawers.

Leschenko stayed on the move, hopping on a bus to Regina, where he switched hotels every night. He left his girlfriend behind at the Holiday Inn shortly before noon on July 27 when he walked to the nearby Toronto-Dominion Bank in the Avon Shopping Centre. Armed with his stolen revolver when he walked up to the two tellers to make a withdrawal, Leschenko left with a paper bag stuffed with $5,340 and the bank's manager and assistant manager running after him. They flagged down RCMP officer Constable Ken Ross, who happened to be driving by, to join the chase.

Leschenko ran into a car sales lot and into a parked vehicle, spilling money to the street from the burst bag. The wanted man kept on going through to the Regina Cemetery, hoping to get lost behind the headstones as more city police officers joined in the chase.

Seeing the commotion, an off-duty officer pulled his car to a stop, bolted from the vehicle before taking his key out of the ignition, and pulled Leschenko out from under a pile of lumber in the yard of a business selling cemetery monuments. The cop and the robber, who each had ahold of the other, were about midway to the off-duty officer's private car before he realized Leschenko had a gun. They separated, and Leschenko raised his pistol and pulled the trigger.

Constable Dave Quick, one of the officers in the chase, saw the dirt kick up and the man go down. "He just shot the guy!" Quick yelled into his police radio.

Leschenko jumped into the idling 1967 Oldsmobile, then hesitated. Having spent so much of his short life behind bars, he was confused by an automatic and searched for the clutch.

One officer took aim with his .38 Special and sent a bullet through the window and into Leschneko's belly. He still managed to put the stolen car into gear—first instead

Photo of stolen vehicle involved in chase and shootout, 1973. Photographer: Ian Caldwell, courtesy Regina *Leader-Post*.

of drive—and lean on the gas. A hail of some 20 police bullets shattered the windows and riddled the car's metal with holes. One more bullet, crashing through the glass, caught Leschenko's left shoulder. It didn't stop him or the fleeing Oldsmobile.

As the car sped away, Quick ran to check on the fallen officer. He miraculously rose to his feet. "My God, are you all right?" asked Quick.

"What the hell happened?" replied the stunned officer. When he had seen Leschenko raise his pistol, the cop had shoved the robber. As the gun fired, the officer's knees buckled and he dropped to the ground. It probably saved his life.

He and Quick jumped in another car with a pair of detectives to join the chase. The police radio crackled with directions and street names like Albert, Pasqua, Kings, and ultimately 23rd Avenue and Hillsdale.

Officer Jim Ralston and his partner were at the head of a line of police cars in hot pursuit on a Friday afternoon in late July, from one end of the city to the other in mere minutes. Ralston watched as Leschenko's fleeing car narrowly missed a cyclist. One bridge worker jumped in a creek to get clear of the string of speeding vehicles. Dust clouded the air when the chase veered onto a yet-to-be paved road, sending one police cruiser careening into parked cars.

The chase ended when Leschenko also crashed, losing control of the Oldsmobile on a median. Quick and Ralston were among the first officers to reach the stolen car. Leschenko, losing blood but not quite consciousness, was slumped behind the wheel. His .357 Magnum was no longer in his hand.

Leschenko went to the hospital for surgery, then back to prison. Police found $760 of the stolen money in the car. It and about $4,000 retrieved by honest bystanders when the robber dropped his loot was returned to the bank. Another $600 found in Leschenko's hotel room eventually went back to the bank in Calgary.

A judge sentenced Leschenko, then 22 years old, to a further 10 years on top of the 12 years he had been serving before he went AWOL from prison. He is an intelligent young man, defence lawyer Mark Mulatz urged the judge, and might yet succeed in turning his life around.

Less than a year later, Leschenko got another six months tacked on to his sentence for attempting to escape from the Saskatchewan Penitentiary.

His next former address was Millhaven, a maximum-security prison in Ontario. Leschenko and his fellow inmate from the escape in British Columbia were joined by a third prisoner in their bid for freedom just a few days before Christmas in 1975. After cutting through the bars on the windows, the trio wrapped themselves in white sheets and disappeared into a heavy snowstorm.

Freedom lasted two months before Leschenko was arrested in Florida for another bank robbery and threatening violence. He had spent nearly three years in an American prison, of his 15-year US sentence, when he was returned to Canada to serve his time for crimes on both sides of the border. In April 1980, he escaped again. His one day of freedom added another year to his burgeoning sentence.

Four years later, he didn't need to escape; Leschenko simply walked away. Given an unescorted pass and $300 from the Edmonton Institution, Leschenko was supposed to go and register for a university class. He was arrested less than a month later in Las Vegas after pulling another bank robbery.

He slipped away again, this time making it as far as Hawaii, where he bought and operated a parasailing business. Almost a year to the day after his Las Vegas arrest, Leschenko was busted in Hawaii, stopped for driving violations. He escaped again—briefly. In January 1986, Leschenko was sentenced to 39 years for four counts of armed robbery and two of escape.

Leschenko's revolving prison doors closed firmly at that point. There was an attempt to escape in 1990 from the prison in Leavenworth, Kansas, but the next change of address wasn't what he had in mind. Leschenko was transferred to Marion prison in Illinois, a so-called "supermaximum" secure facility for the Houdini-like escape artist. When he was paroled in the States, Leschenko was handed over to immigration officials and returned to a Canadian prison in 2008 to finish his sentence.

Prison authorities in Canada refused to give Leschenko credit on his Canadian sentence for the time served in Uncle Sam's big house. He took his fight to the courts, but couldn't get a two-for-one discount. "The time during which a prisoner is unlawfully at large," a federal court judge ruled, "does not count as part of his term of imprisonment."

No longer a young man at age 58, Leschenko told parole officials in 2009 he was a changed man, done with escaping after realizing it wasn't getting him anywhere. But the parole board was unimpressed with his vague plans to find room and board and some sort of job with computers. He remained in prison.

Leschenko took another run at the courts three years later, trying to find a legal loophole through which he could slip away before his sentence expires in 2022. "Thirty-nine years of relatively continuous incarceration has been an adequate deterrent and continued incarceration serves no legitimate penal purpose," Leschenko argued without success.

His last known address was the Drumheller Institution.

ONE OF THE BEST KILLING ROOMS

Her father was a killer.

Bob Dyer worked on the killing floor, in a room spattered with dried chicken blood and covered by the feathers that stuck to it. Ropes hung from the ceiling, each cord ending in a small piece of wood from which to suspend the slaughtered poultry. The stench of the blood and wet feathers wasn't as bad in the winter, when the icy chill left frost on the sheet metal that covered the lower half of the walls. Still, despite the cold, the unmistakable smell of death clung to the air in the killing room.

That's where they found Elsie Dyer. Her 14-year-old body lay near the centre of the room, as if she was asleep in the six-inch-deep carpet of dirty white feathers that covered the floor. She wore a black dress, brown stockings, and a white sweater with a thin black-and-red band at the waistline and neck. She had on the brown overshoes and fur jacket that she had pulled on the night before when she left her home on an errand for her father. Elsie had showed up at Charlie Morley's filling station and shop around 7:45 that evening to pick up a pouch of tobacco for her father. She smiled but didn't make much conversation with clerk Karl Forbes, who watched her leave with her purchase. She walked north in the direction of her 25th Street home, two blocks away. But somehow she ended up across the street from Morley's in the padlocked packing plant.

Elsie's pretty face was smeared with blood and feathers, her right eye was swollen and blackened, and her nose was broken. Even worse were the blows—to her forehead, slightly above her neck at the back of her head, and in front of her right ear—that had fractured her skull and violently ended her young life.

It was Elsie's father who found his battered daughter in the killing room on March 15, 1935. Robert "Bob" Bernard Dyer had lost his job in December when Continental Packers closed up its Saskatoon plant at Avenue D and 23rd Street. He had worked there since moving from Prince Albert some two years earlier. Bob was determined there was still money to be made in the poultry business, despite the Depression, and he partnered with former co-worker Russell Adams in a plan to reopen. Russell and Bob had spent the previous week cleaning up the plant in preparation for their new venture. They had not gotten to the killing room by March 14, having to wait for it to thaw so they could clean up the frozen feathers and blood.

Roused by Bob on March 15, Russell drove Bob and his wife to Elsie's school early that morning to see if anyone might know where she could have gone. The inquiries met with no success. Finally, around 9:30 that morning, Bob suggested to his business partner that they might as well go to the plant and get some work done. Opening the padlock on the door, Bob took about three or four steps into the main room when he noticed something on the floor, between the stove and the entrance to the killing room. "There is the tobacco I sent her for," he exclaimed, picking up a packet of Ogden's Fine Cut.

Frantically rushing around the plant, Bob looked behind the rows of poultry crates that filled the main floor and peered into corners. He opened the door to the killing room and took the two stairs down to the floor. Crying hysterically, he ran towards Elsie's body.

Three days later, the schoolgirl was buried in a small white coffin. Neither her father nor her mother attended the funeral at St. Paul's Cathedral, where several of Elsie's former classmates filled the seats. Katherine Dyer had reportedly taken to her bed after suffering a breakdown. And Bob Dyer became so overwrought upon viewing his child's body before the funeral that he was taken back home. "I want to be with my little girl," he was heard crying as he left the funeral home.

A pathologist determined Elsie had been killed by a blunt force instrument, like a metal bar, perhaps even from the ironworks yard next door to the packing plant. What neither he nor the police could say was who had wielded it or why. Besides the brutal beating, there was no sign the girl had been violated.

Elsie had been in grade six at St. Paul's School, which she attended with her 10-year-old sister, Mellie. Elsie's teacher knew her as quiet and shy, but she was friendly with her playmates. To her parents, she was an obedient child. Before leaving on the errand for her father, Elsie had cleaned up the supper dishes, then sought her mother's help in sewing a dress. The girl was in the midst of ripping off the overly large sleeves when her father asked her to go to the store for him.

"Yes Daddy, I'll go, and we'll finish the dress when I come back," Elsie had said.

When Elsie didn't return, her father went looking for her at the store, where he was told she had left nearly an hour earlier. Further inquiries were made with friends. Her mother would later tell police she had assumed Elsie had maybe stopped by Bill's Lunch Room, where her aunt worked. Or perhaps she'd gone to a picture show. That's why they didn't immediately call police. But when Elsie still wasn't home by midnight, Mr. Dyer, who didn't have a phone at the rooming house where the family lived, walked over to the car barns to call police and report the girl's disappearance.

The police were stumped. The only lead seemed to be some passing motorists who had seen what appeared to be a man and a woman entering the packing plant between 8:30 and 9:00 at night on March 14. There were only two keys to the padlocked door—one kept by McKee Cartage Company, from whom the building was leased, and the other by Bob Dyer.

Bob would testify at a coroner's inquest that he and his wife had indeed gone into the packing plant on March 14.

Returning home after his stop by Morley's store, he had told his wife to put on her coat and come with him to the plant. The family's little dog, which they'd gotten at Christmas, accompanied them. Mrs. Dyer let the fox terrier off its leash to run around the building. Mr. Dyer said he showed his wife the killing room, and he told the jury about the pile of feathers pushed up towards the north end of the room. His wife also had experience in chicken-killing work, and Bob recalled her commenting on the room. He turned off the light, Mrs. Dyer put the dog back on the leash, and they left the plant, padlocking the door behind them.

The next day, he found his daughter's body. "I could see her plain enough, if that's what you want to know," he told the inquest between his sobs. "That's as far as I can go. She wasn't hidden from me."

Asked if Elsie had any enemies, her father replied: "I've thought that out until I'm crazy, and I can't think of anyone. I don't know who might have had a motive."

Nor could Elsie's mother think of anyone who wanted her child dead. "I cannot picture anyone so cruel that I know of," she said. Mrs. Dyer was emphatic: "Elsie never went into that building alive."

Dressed in a black hat and black fur coat, Katherine Dyer took the stand 10 minutes after her husband. She remembered spending most of March 14 on the chesterfield because of a headache. She clearly recalled that they had warmed-over vegetables, rice pudding with fruit, cake, bread and butter, and tea for supper. Ordinarily, she wouldn't have left the house because she had washed her hair. But when Bob returned from the store, he suggested they take a walk to look for Elsie. And if they didn't encounter her, they could go to the plant and he could show her the progress made in cleaning it out, she said.

Mrs. Dyer recalled seeing the mass of feathers on the killing room floor and blood on the walls. She had remarked on what a fine killing room it was. "It is one of the best killing rooms you've had," she told her husband.

Our Cir. No. 17,
April 26, 1935. **SASKATOON POLICE DEPARTMENT**

$500 (Five Hundred Dollars) Reward
MURDER

I am authorized by the City Council of the City of Saskatoon to offer a reward of $500.00 for information leading to the arrest and conviction of the person or persons responsible for the murder of ELSIE DYER, 320 25th Street West, Saskatoon, Sask.

The body of Elsie Dyer, 14½-year-old Saskatoon girl, was found in the Continental Packing Plant, 319 23rd Street W., Saskatoon, at about 9.30 a.m. March 15, 1935. The girl had apparently been murdered at about 8.00 p.m. on the 14th March, 1935, death being due to four wounds on back, front and side of head.

This reward shall not be payable to any Police Officer in the Province of Saskatchewan.

In the event of there being more than one claimant for the said reward, it shall be apportioned as the Chief Constable, Saskatoon, deems just.

Police Departments may wire me any information collect.

SASKATOON POLICE HEADQUARTERS,
SASKATOON, SASK., CANADA,

APRIL 26, 1935.

GEORGE M. DONALD,
CHIEF CONSTABLE.

Reward poster issued in the Elsie Dyer homicide, circa 1935. Source: Department of the Attorney General files, Saskatchewan Archives Board, R-321-file 6.7.

But what neither of the Dyers could say was how they could have missed Elsie's body if indeed it had been there that night.

"When we left the plant, we were fully confident that she would be home," Mrs. Dyer said.

The verdict by the coroner's jury came as no surprise. Elsie had been murdered "by person or persons unknown."

A month after Elsie's death, the City of Saskatoon offered a reward of $500 for information leading to an arrest and conviction in her murder. It was never collected. During a prayer service that April, an evangelist minister delivered a sermon titled "Who Killed Elsie Dyer?" Mrs. Dyer sent a message to the minister after the service and asked to say a few words. She suggested there were people in Saskatoon who knew more about the murder than they were willing to tell—and she appealed for them to step forward.

Finding it impossible to live any longer in Saskatoon in the shadow of suspicion, the Dyers decided to relocate to Prince Albert. As they prepared to board the train on May 18, 1935, the Dyers told a *Star-Phoenix* reporter how they could no longer tolerate the "unjust accusations." That same month, they collected on an insurance policy for Elsie's death. Taken out in July 1933, the policy had a value of $450 and paid double indemnity in the event of an accident or foul play.

"Everywhere we go, we have the finger of suspicion pointed at us," Bob Dyer told the reporter. "The last two months have been too much for my wife. We have been hounded all the time."

Katherine Dyer reiterated that she knew nothing more about Elsie's death. "My husband and I visited that packing plant at nine o'clock the night that Elsie disappeared. She was not there then, no matter how much people say she was. She was not there."

"Even after I heard that she was dead, I thought she must have been hit by a car. Such a thing as—well—as the thing that happened never occurred to me," continued Mrs. Dyer. "I don't know why anyone should do anything to her. She was a good girl."

---

*In February 1937, the lawyer hired by the Attorney General to oversee prosecution of the case sent a bill for $200 and closed his file, given a lack of direct evidence to lay charges. Elsie's slaying remains unsolved.

DETERMINATION

Well past lunchtime, Mary notices the blinds are still drawn at her neighbour's house. Earlier, as Mary had sat with her morning coffee around 5:30, she had noticed a light on at the house. Irene, who lived alone, was normally a later riser. Yet Mary had glimpsed someone come out of the house at that time. She thought it was Irene and wondered if perhaps something was wrong with the furnace. Mary dressed in preparation to go and offer a hand to the 81-year-old widow. But when Mary looked out again, the lights at Irene's house were off and the blinds drawn. She's probably gone back to bed, thought Mary. Now, several hours later, the shades are still down.

Deciding to go and check, Mary opens her neighbour's door to find the house black with smoke. Mary notices the bed in Irene's room has been stripped of its sheets and blankets. Mary's son goes to the basement to check on the furnace and suddenly calls to his mother. He has found Irene.

She is unconscious, lying on her back at the bottom of the stairs. Coated with black soot, the elderly woman is dressed in her nightgown and covered by a tangle of scorched blankets. Blood mats her white hair, and her left arm appears broken. It looks like some terrible accident.

Except nylon stockings bind Irene's feet and hands.

* * *

His words come fast and his voice is smooth, like a good salesman. But the younger man across from him isn't buying his pitch. Not for now, anyway.

"I'm here for you tonight," Roger tells Terry. "We all make mistakes. I'm no different," he adds. "I don't bullshit people … I like talking just common sense."

Silence.

Roger tries again to win over the man. "We're all the same people," he continues. Roger is understanding, easygoing, even likeable—just one of the guys. He's different from the other man, the one with the harder edge to his voice who talked to Terry first. He accused Terry of things and called him a liar. Terry told him his lawyer had directed him not to talk. And Terry is steadfastly determined that he is going to follow that advice. Terry gives Roger the same message.

"It's easy for people to tell you to say nothing." His tone is even and conversational, as though they are buddies chatting at the bar.

"If two men sit down and get an incident like this straightened out, isn't that what life's about?" he asks. Roger says he understands—no car, a cold night, nowhere to go. If you took a hundred people and put them in the same situation, they'd probably react the same way, he assures Terry. "You simply went there to warm up," he adds.

Finally, he's rewarded with at least a monosyllabic answer: "Uh hum," says Terry. That's progress.

Roger presses on. "When you went to the house, you didn't plan to hurt anybody." He assures the young man he wouldn't be mad if someone came into his house to warm up and didn't wreck the place. "Did you go to that house to hurt anybody?" he asks.

When there's no response, Roger answers for him. "No," he says, working hard to win the man's confidence. "We're equals. We're two men.

"I tell people, for Christ's sake, tell me what happened," says Roger. "Tell me your side of the story."

As the minutes stretch into hours, Terry's single-word

responses grow to full sentences. And the sentences grow more telling.

Roger offers encouragement as needed. "It's a breath of fresh air to run into a person that's on the same wavelength as me," he says. "If a guy's in a bit of shit—a bit of a bind—let's talk about it. What do you do?"

"Tell the truth," replies Terry.

Their conversation will last two and a half hours. By the end of it, Terry is talking. A lot. "I'm glad you came down here," he tells Roger.

He's still talking the next day when he goes back to the house in Lipton, this time with a video camera and a crew of Mounties to watch him re-enact what he's done.

"From things that I've learned from other people," Terry tells them as he draws to a close, "you know, if you're going to do a crime, you might as well not leave any witnesses. So I thought burning down the house would solve that for me."

* * *

Irene awakens sometime after 3:30 in the morning to a terrible pain radiating from the back of her head. She feels something wet and realizes blood is seeping from a cut.

Hard of hearing, Irene reaches over and switches on a lamp as she tries to sort out what's occurred. The light reveals a man seated on the end of her bed. He has a metal bar, shaped like the number seven, in his hands. That barely registers before the stranger swings the tire iron at her again.

Irene grabs at the weapon and tussles with the intruder, not quite a third her age. She slides off the bed, and he falls down on top of her. When the tenacious senior tries to bite one of the man's hands, he smashes a glass vase over her head.

Everything goes black.

When Irene comes to, the intruder's hands under her nightgown reveal that he's intent on stealing more than property. He drags her to the foot of the bed, covers her face with the bedspread, and takes what he wants from the senior.

Irene's body feels paralyzed, and again she passes out.

When she awakens this time, Irene gingerly peers out the bedroom doorway, looking for an escape. But he sees her and returns to the bedroom to bind her hands and feet with her nylon stockings. Confident he's managed to subdue the woman, he leaves her alone.

Undeterred, Irene seizes the opportunity. She works at the stretchy bindings until she's able to free both of her hands and one foot. Reaching for her scissors, she cuts the nylons off her other foot. Irene steps out of her bedroom, catches a glimpse of denim pants in the bathroom—and runs.

He catches her just as she gets the back door unlocked and drags her back. Irene lashes out with the scissors still clutched in her hands. But he is merciless, and twists the old woman's left arm until it breaks. She feels his hands around her neck and passes out.

Irene comes to as her head bumps down each of the stairs of the split-level. He's dragging her to the basement. As Irene, her hands and feet bound once again, struggles, he throws blankets pulled from the bedroom on top her. He lights a piece of paper on the stove and tosses the burning material on the blankets. He returns to the kitchen for a glass of water, careful to wipe his prints off of it. The man takes his jacket and $22 of Irene's money, then walks out the back door. A block away, he deposits the tire iron with the woman's blood on it into a garbage bin.

Alone, Irene watches in terror as flames reach a foot high and thinks about the nearby gas furnace.

* * *

Quite a few people notice the bloodstains on Terry Bear's grey bunny hug sweater that Saturday, October 15, 1994. Terry chalks it up to a fight at the bar. One of the guys teases him about getting blamed for that break-in everyone is talking about, the one at the old woman's house early that morning.

"It wasn't me," says Terry.

But later, while headed down the highway with his buddies, Terry pulls off the sweater and flings it out the car window from his place in the back seat. He had wanted to stop at the nuisance grounds and burn the stained shirt, but it was Saturday night, and they were anxious to get to town for beer.

It's December when Terrence Lester Bear sits across from Roger Wigglesworth, not at the bar but in an interview room. The RCMP sergeant wants to talk about that blood people saw on Terry's sweater. Wigglesworth makes it easy for Terry to talk, downplaying the crime, assuring Terry he's probably a good guy at heart, and making other offenders seem far worse by comparison. As if he is putting together building blocks, Wigglesworth starts small and gradually works up. Terry's determination to keep quiet falters. He goes from admitting he went inside simply to warm up to telling how he pried open a basement window with the tire iron, removed his shoes after crawling inside so he could creep quietly around, struck the homeowner with a tire iron, raped her, tied her up, and tried to kill the woman so as not to leave any witnesses.

Irene proved far more determined.

As she lay on the basement floor, expecting to be consumed by fire, the woman who had wrestled with an intruder armed with a tire iron, who had managed to escape from the bonds he had tied, who had tried to bite him and lash out at him with her scissors, who had come fleetingly close to freedom only to be beaten and bound again now fought for her life.

From somewhere, a bloodied and battered Irene found the strength to roll around, as best she could with her bound limbs and broken arm, to smother the flames. She also somehow managed to open up a gallon jug of water stored by the furnace, and knock it over to douse any remaining flames before she passed out.

"I guess God was with me," the amazingly resilient woman would later tell a jury at the trial of Terrence Lester Bear. Irene couldn't describe her attacker. She couldn't even point him out in the courtroom.

Terry Bear, 1995. Photographer: Bob Watson, courtesy Regina *Leader-Post.*

But her blood was on Terry Bear's tattered bunny hug, recovered from the ditch by the Mounties. And his denials on the witness stand rang hollow against his videotaped confession with Wigglesworth, the re-enactment of his crimes at Irene's house, his demonstration of how he ditched the tire iron, and his identification of the sweater with the blood on the front and the picture of a sailboat on the back.

Terry was his own worst witness.

Convicted of aggravated sexual assault and attempted murder, Bear was spared a life sentence because of Irene. "He did everything he could to kill her," Crown prosecutor Alistair Johnston told the court, "and he will get a lot of credit because she refused to die."

In March 1996, Justice Ron Barclay sentenced Bear to 20 years in prison and ordered him to serve half that term, instead of the usual third, before being eligible to seek parole.

"If it wasn't for the courage, self-determination, tenacity and strength of an extraordinary lady, you would have been facing a murder charge," Barclay said.

Terry was 28 years old when he walked into Irene's house; he is 43 when he walks out of prison. He has learned a few things in that time—about his crime, about himself. Terry believes the rage inside of him stems from his own abuse as a child and from witnessing other family members being hurt. Terry tells the parole officials he will not drink anymore, he is going to take psychological counselling, and he intends to stay out of trouble.

He is determined.

*The names Irene and Mary are pseudonyms. A court-imposed publication ban protects the identity of the victim.

LOVERS' WHISPERS

It seemed as though they'd been up half the night, talking and giggling. Lovers' whispers that floated through the thin walls into the bedroom where Frank lay trying to sleep.

Margaret was sitting on top of the woodbox and George was in the rocking chair. An oil lamp burned yellow and warm on the table between them.

Margaret and George had been engaged since the fall of 1927, nearly two years by then, and they planned to marry in the spring. After that, Margaret could move out of the Carriers' home, and she and George would have a place of their own.

Margaret was looking forward to the move.

The Carriers' home was a small log cabin in the country north of North Battleford, cramped and close with five adults and two small children living there—with thin walls that carried sound, and Frank with a lousy temper.

Frank and his wife had gone to bed before seven. Frank's son and daughter-in law and their kids retired to the room they all shared a little while after that.

Margaret and George stayed up, giggling together in the lamplight.

Suddenly, Frank shouted at them from his bedroom.

"You two get out of here," he yelled.

"Mind your own business," George yelled back. "I don't have to get out."

Through the thin wall, Margaret and George heard the old man get out of bed and move around the small room in short, shuffling footsteps. Everything was quiet for a moment, and Margaret wondered if Frank had gone back to bed.

Then they heard a clicking noise.

Then a sound like shells being loaded into the chamber of a gun.

George whispered: "Does he have a gun in there?"

"I don't know," said Margaret.

The bedroom door burst open. Frank Carrier stood fully dressed in trousers, a coat, boots, and a hat, with a gun in his hands. He pointed the barrel directly at George, who hadn't moved from the rocking chair.

"Now get out, damn you," Frank said in a growl. "I will show you whether you will get out, you damned dirty outlaw."

George stared at the gun. He didn't have time to move before the first bullet hit, tearing into the flesh and bone of his right shoulder.

The moment they heard the shot, Dave and Myrtle jumped out of bed. Dave knew it was his father.

"My God," he said. "What's happening now?"

As he ran out of his bedroom, Dave saw George Dawson standing in the doorway before him, his face pale in the moonlit night. "He shot me," George said, a stain of wet red blood growing on his shoulder.

Then came a second shot. George fell face down to the floor.

Frank ran from the house, disappearing quickly into the darkness.

While Margaret and Dave knelt around the injured man, Myrtle put on her shoes and her kimono.

"You do as much as you can for George and I will go," she told her husband.

Myrtle ran to her father's farm nearby, where she mounted a horse and road bareback to the telephone office to call the doctor.

But George was already beyond the doctor's help.

He lay on the floor in a growing pool of blood, his eyes dull and unfocused and his skin deathly pale. Margaret washed her sweetheart's face with cold water as he drew his final breath.

Frank showed up at his friend Gordon Palmer's house the next morning. The old man was tired and ragged, still carrying the gun.

"Give yourself up," Gordon told Frank.

"I don't know what to do," Frank said. "I guess they will hang me."

"No. They won't hang you at all, if you give yourself up," Gordon said. "You will have a good chance."

When Gordon asked Frank for the gun and the cartridge, Frank handed them over without argument. The men ate supper together, and then headed towards Meadow Lake so Frank could turn himself in.

They met RCMP Constable A. J. Stretton on the road.

"Is George dead?" Frank asked the officer.

"He is," Stretton replied. "He is dead."

"I'm kind of sorry," Frank said. "But that damned outlaw deserved it."

* * *

The shooting wasn't a surprise to many people in the area, who knew Frank Carrier to be a man of violent temper who had threatened to shoot other people in the past.

"He was generally feared," an RCMP crime report noted. "It was generally expected that sooner or later he would kill someone."

One neighbour, who had known Frank for more than a decade, remembered telling his wife: "Something is going to happen."

Before the trial, the superintendent of the North Battleford Mental Hospital wondered whether Frank's advanced age might have played a role in the killing, noting that it was "generally conceded that men are not as bright when they are old and feeble as they are when they are young."

Still, after meeting with Frank, the doctor found him to be in good condition. He said he believed Frank knew right from wrong when he shot George, and that the signs of senility Frank sometimes showed were not a concern.

"We all have that," the doctor said. "I have that myself."

* * *

The trial took place early in 1929. Among the key witnesses were George Dawson's fiancé, Margaret, and several members of Frank Carrier's own family.

Henry Carrier testified that his father had once gone to jail for hitting Henry's wife in the head with a gun, and described his father as having "about as high a temper as a man could have."

Henry said his family had long been concerned about Frank's potential for violence.

"He is different from any other man I ever seen," Henry said, as his father sat in the prisoner's box across the courtroom. "I can get along with everybody I ever met, but I never could satisfy him."

Frank himself had already acknowledged his own bad temper to the RCMP, telling one officer: "I know I am quick tempered but have always tried hard to keep myself in hand."

He had also fully confessed to shooting George Dawson, saying: "I let the gun go. I shot him. I was kind of sorry afterwards, but I had enough of him."

The jury took little time in finding Frank Carrier guilty of murder, and he was sentenced to death by hanging. The execution was set for May 1929.

But the notion of executing an old man did not sit well with many members of the Canadian public.

Frank's cause was taken up by the Canadian Prisoners' Welfare Association, which sent a letter urging that the condemned man be granted special consideration because of his age.

"The fact of a man who has reached the psalmists' allotted span of life being hanged seems repugnant to most minds, and it would seem that if this man were sent to the penitentiary and were to die in the institution in the course of nature the purposes of justice would be sufficiently served."

Another man who wrote a letter opposing the execution said hanging an old man would be "a blot and a black eye" on Canadian justice.

As the date of Frank's death approached, the date of his birth proved to be a matter of some question.

Frank initially told the police he was 63. To the trial judge, he looked 65. Henry Carrier thought his father was 68. Frank's lawyer said his client was 76. Frank's other son, Dave, was so confused about his father's age he wouldn't even hazard a guess.

Not even Frank seemed to know how old he was.

"I don't know my age exactly," Frank said, "but according to what I was told a long time ago by my parents, I should be 76 years of age now."

* * *

However many years it had lasted, Frank Carrier's life had not been an easy one. His father was killed in a bar fight not long after Frank was born. When his mother died a few years later, the orphaned Frank was sent to New Brunswick to live with a family he had never met and didn't like.

As a teenager, Frank ran away to his grandfather's house and found work as a lumberjack.

"I never had a day's schooling in my life," he would say later. "As soon as a boy grew up big enough to handle an axe in those days we had to start in working and schools were not bothered with."

In jail, he lamented that he had never had a chance to help his mind with books or learning.

As officials worked to determine his true age before the execution, Frank lived well in prison. To the guards, he came to be known as a polite and "most gentlemanly old fellow,"

Frank Carrier. Copyright Government of Canada. Reproduced with the permission of the Minister of Public Works and Government Services Canada (2013). Source: Library and Archives Canada/Department of Justice fonds/e10900376.

who spoke in clean, courteous and kindly language, and didn't blame anyone else for the trouble he was in.

The guards said Frank was in good spirits most of the time, and didn't seem overly concerned that he'd killed George Dawson, or that he had been sentenced to die.

A certificate of baptism uncovered in Frenchville, Maine, confirmed that Frank was born on January 11, 1865, making him 64. His real name was Fortuna.

Shortly before Frank was to be executed, his sentence was commuted to life imprisonment. News of the commutation came around the same time George and Margaret were supposed to have been married.

Frank applied for a ticket of leave to get out of prison the next year, and twice a year after that. He was always denied.

"I am a man 77 years of age, and would like to spend what time I have left to live with my wife on the farm," he wrote in 1933.

Pleading for release in 1937, Frank wrote: "I am getting old and weaker. I would like to go out and help my family."

Deathly ill with tuberculosis and diabetes, Frank was finally granted release from the prison in 1938—but only to be transferred to Holy Family Hospital, where he died a short time later.

"The next of kin was notified, but made no claim for the body," Warden H. W. Cooper wrote in a note on Carrier's file. "Carrier was therefore buried in the Penitentiary cemetery at 1100 hours on Tuesday, August 9."

He was 73.

THE CHASE

A noise coming from behind the warehouse shortly after midnight caught the officer's ear. The patrolman was making his rounds on the beat that Friday. He moved in for a closer look behind the Texas Oil Company of Canada and spotted George Fodor. The young man was hunched down, surrounded by three tires complete with rims and tubes. He had been in the midst of helping himself to a fourth tire on the trailer until interrupted by the Regina policeman. Fodor didn't waste any time. Jumping to his feet, he took off at a sprint, leading the officer on a wild chase through back lots, down alleys, and over fences for a full half mile.

Despite having the advantage of youth, Fodor still wasn't any match for an eager, slim, fit, young constable, who scaled an eight-foot fence at one point in the pursuit. The officer would later tell his mother how he couldn't have done it, but for wearing his lighter shoes that night.

Caught red-handed, the 21-year-old fugitive had few options when he appeared that morning, August 4, 1933, in police court before Magistrate R. E. Turnbull. The charge was theft.

"Guilty," Fodor replied when asked for his plea. Turnbull put off sentencing until after the weekend.

The constable's mother, Mrs. E. Lenhard, was still talking about her son George's exploits that Sunday when she visited with Mrs. E. J. Gaetz. Mrs. Lenhard, who was staying at her son's apartment, couldn't be prouder of her boy and the chase that had made the front page of the newspaper the same day as his 28th birthday. A former teacher and welder, he had been on the force not quite three years and was already making a name for himself.

The two women were still visiting in the parlour of Mrs. Gaetz's home that evening when a neighbour boy came to the door. He delivered news that would keep the name of Constable George Anthony Lenhard in the headlines for days and years to come.

Mrs. Lenhard easily read the expression on Mrs. Gaetz face when she returned to the parlour.

"Tell me, what is it?" said Mrs. Lenhard.

Mrs. Gaetz could barely form the words: "It's George. He's been hurt."

* * *

Constable Lenhard was out on patrol in much the same area where he had stumbled upon Fodor. Some 45 minutes into his night shift on August 6, the officer was riding a bicycle to check on businesses in a sprawling area of warehouses, small industrial plants, and open prairie along the rail line.

As he came upon the Canadian Liquid Air Plant, at Winnipeg Street and Fourth Avenue, a man caught the officer's keen eye. It was nearing 10:00 p.m., and the shabbily dressed stranger in dark clothing didn't appear to have any legitimate business in the area. Lenhard turned his bicycle to follow. Two other men, similarly dressed, stepped out of the shadows behind the constable. Lenhard was standing beside his bicycle, hands holding the bars, when he called for the man in front of him to halt.

The man turned to reveal a .32-calibre automatic pistol in his hand, pointed at Lenhard.

"Stick 'em up," he shouted at the officer.

"What?" replied the stunned junior constable, moving back towards the brick wall of the warehouse as the gunman pursued him. The first bullet went clean through Lenhard's right arm just below the armpit.

Constable George Lenhard. Source: Regina Police Service museum.

Two more shots echoed in the night as Lenhard was backed up against the wall with the help of the other two men. One bullet pierced the front of the officer's tunic, entered his right breast, and severed a major artery before emerging through his back. Another got him in the back, slicing through the top of his heart before exiting out the front, on the left side of his chest. That bullet never tore the front of his uniform, leading the coroner, Dr. W. A. Thomson, to offer the opinion that the shot had come as Lenhard opened his tunic to reach for his own revolver.

Lenhard was the force's best shot with a revolver, winning the Bruton Cup that year. But his gun never left its holster that night. There simply was not any time to get it out from under his tunic.

The three men ran off into the darkness—the gunman sprinting behind the British America Oil plant across the street and the two accomplices down Fourth Avenue—as the dying officer crawled along the side of the warehouse. He saw an overhead door. Lenhard struggled to get onto the raised platform beneath the opening and force the door upwards.

Inside the plant where he worked as an acetylene operator, Lloyd Draper had heard the popping sounds—and chalked them up to kids playing with firecrackers. He was on his way to tell the kids to move along when the officer, covered with blood, rolled through the door.

Draper rushed to the officer's side. Lenhard mumbled two incomprehensible words and collapsed.

Lenhard's pulse was fading when some of his fellow officers arrived minutes later. They were carrying him to the ambulance when one officer said, "He's gone."

Father Peter Hughes broke the news to Lenhard's mother.

"My poor boy," she sobbed. "My darling boy. He was such a good boy. He wouldn't have hurt anyone for the world."

Lenhard was the first Regina police officer killed in the line of duty.

Mounties, railway police, retired officers, and special constables who had just spent two weeks patrolling the World's Grain Show on the exhibition grounds and a tent city created for it joined members of the Regina police force in the hunt for the killers. Local residents, including Mayor James McAra, turned over their vehicles for use in the search. More than three hundred transients—picked up from freight cars in the railway yards, from around the exhibition grounds, and from vacant lots—were hauled into the police station for questioning. The vague descriptions of the wanted men—a gunman who was tall and heavy-set, and the two accomplices, who were younger and smaller, all dressed like hobos—could have easily fit hundreds of men wandering the city, between the Depression and the exhibition.

On Monday, as more than a hundred officers searched for Lenhard's killers, Magistrate Turnbull presided over police court.

"I would like to say a word of tribute to an officer who has met death while on duty," he said as that day's proceedings got under way. "He was a capable and conscientious police officer, and a good citizen. And I am sure we all regret his passing."

The last man arrested by Lenhard was on the docket that morning. Turnbull sentenced Fodor, the thief who had been unable to outrun the diligent officer three days earlier, to a month in jail.

For decades, police chased tips about Lenhard's killers, but the law never caught up to the men responsible.

HALF-BAKED

At 78 years of age, Julia was known to suffer from the occasional "weak spell." The one that took hold that Friday evening, however, seemed much worse than usual. It worried her husband, Karl Schindler, to the point that he pulled open the door of their home and began to shout for help. But Karl himself also wasn't very well.

Neighbours, hearing the cries of the 86-year-old, rushed to his aid. He was staggering in the doorway and appeared to have slipped and fallen on the ice outside the couple's home in Hubbard. Now the elderly man was in pain and unable to walk. Karl was laid out in one room and his wife in the other when the doctor arrived from nearby Ituna. But there was very little he could do. The devoted husband and wife died within 10 minutes of each other. The doctor attributed the deaths to natural causes, perhaps stroke or heart failure, maybe shock.

The Schindlers were Russian immigrants who had settled in the Hubbard area in 1903. In their retirement, the aging farm couple had mentioned to a few people that as they lived for one another, they hoped one day to die together. For that reason, their deaths on December 20, 1935, were initially seen as a bittersweet tragedy. "Death, Calling Twice in 10 Minutes, Grants Desire of Aged Hubbard Pair," read the headline in the *Saskatoon Star-Phoenix* the next day.

But in the days and months that followed, a terrible, unsavoury truth began to emerge.

When John, the Schindlers' adult son who lived with his parents, left the house that evening to attend the local Christmas concert, his father was biting into a bran muffin. John had brought home four muffins, but he hadn't had time to eat any of them before leaving for the concert. Packed in a shoebox, the home baking was a Christmas gift John had received earlier in the day. The school concert was barely under way when John and other family members were summoned to the Schindlers' home around 8:00 p.m. John arrived to find his parents in agony, their bodies stiffening and racked by spasms.

"John, there's something wrong," Karl told his son. With his last bit of energy, the elderly man pointed to his vest pocket. John retrieved a roll of bills, some $26, a final gift to a son from his dying father.

Sometime later, after the shock of his parents' sudden death, John noticed that only two of the four bran muffins remained. His sister took them back to her house. When her daughters bit into the muffins, they immediately spit the pieces back out without swallowing because of the peculiar flavour.

Suspicious that there was more than bran in the muffins, the family boxed the remaining buns and sent them to a laboratory in Regina. The lab's findings led to the exhumation of the bodies of Julia and Karl Schindler. Pathologist Dr. Frances McGill found their deaths had been anything but natural. The couple had died of a painful, torturous asphyxia due to strychnine, the same poison found in the bran muffins that had been sent to the lab.

What's more, a dog from the area, its body discovered under two feet of snow about a mile from home, had also died of strychnine poisoning. The dog's life had ended two days before the Schindlers' deaths.

The dog belonged to a family well acquainted with the Schindlers; Della, the lady of the house, was their granddaughter.

Della had made about three batches of muffins on December 19. She had saved some dough from the last batch, intending to make one more dozen after dinner. When she served the muffins to her husband, he remarked on the taste. Sort of bitter.

So when she made the last batch, Della upped the sugar and added some extract. It was either almond or vanilla. She couldn't quite remember which flavouring she had used when everyone started asking questions. Half that batch burned, so she tossed out those muffins. As for the remaining six bran muffins, she boxed up two and sent them along with other Christmas presents to her sister in Summerberry. Della put the last four in a parcel for her father. The next day, she met him at the store in town and passed along the muffins as well as a gift of shaving cream from her sister.

Her sister said she ate her two gift muffins, which arrived in the mail a few days later, without any ill effects.

Della admitted that she had asked an uncle to pick her up some Gopher Cop, a rodent killer containing strychnine, about two weeks earlier. It was to take care of a mouse problem, she said. She also conceded, during a coroner's inquest, that it was possible some of the poison could have accidentally gotten into the extract. Her mother, with whom Della and her husband resided, said she once found the can of Gopher Cop in the wash basin and presumed her grandchildren had placed it there. She tightened the lid and moved it to a more secure place.

But police were convinced there was more to the Schindlers' deaths than a baking error. Della was charged with murdering the couple. She insisted it was the case that was half-baked, and she was innocent.

In October 1936, the "comely, 26-year-old, young woman," as the newspapers described her, was tried in the death of her grandfather. Prosecutor Louis McKim tried to convince the jury the Crown had proven its case beyond a reasonable doubt—that the elderly couple had been killed by poison muffins supplied by their granddaughter. And, he insisted, it was by design, not by accident.

Della never stepped into the witness box, but her lawyer, Frank Wilson, had plenty to say on her behalf. He insisted the

Crown had not proven the strychnine was actually the cause of death. Even if there was poison in the muffins, there was nothing to show Della put it in them or that it was already in the muffins when she delivered them. And, Wilson asked, what was Della's motive to kill her grandparents, or even her father?

But Wilson didn't stop there. He suggested if anyone had a motive, it was Della's mother, who was separated from her husband, John Schindler, and owed him money. Married in 1909, the couple had lived apart for the past six years. John held the mortgage on the farmland of his estranged wife, and she owed him $500. However, Mrs. Schindler maintained that while the debt had been a sore point some five years ago, it hadn't been more recently.

Justice George Taylor also had a few thoughts on the case, and he didn't keep them to himself. He suggested Della's conduct was not consistent with her knowing that the parcel she delivered to her father contained poisoned muffins. He also pointed out that Della's mother hadn't been on speaking terms with her husband, the recipient of the muffins, for a number of years. And she had made only two payments on the mortgage. Taylor added that the only evidence the jury had regarding Della baking the muffins came from her mother.

Della was found not guilty by a jury that deliberated for three hours. The prisoner was set free seven months after her arrest.

A coroner's jury had concluded the Schindlers were poisoned by "person or persons unknown." Whether or not they had been deliberately killed; if the poison was truly intended for their son and not for them at all; who that person or persons might be; or if it was all just a terrible baking accident were never resolved.

For some, it all left a bitter aftertaste.

HUSH

The combined weight of the rocks was more than three times that of the tiny body placed next to them.

Like the day of his death, his birthday is uncertain. He likely came into the world sometime that winter, between December 1969 and April 1970. For two weeks, perhaps even as long as a month, someone provided for his care, ensuring he was fed and kept alive. He was a well-nourished six and a half pounds when he took his last breath. He had beautiful, soft black hair.

There wasn't anything—no marks, no bruises, no broken bones—to show any outward physical sign that he was unloved or unwanted. No, it was, if anything, quite the opposite. Someone had taken the time to put on his cloth diaper and plastic pants, clothe him in his sleeper, give him his soother, and wrap him in a blanket—the careful preparations for an outing.

Except the baby was then packed in a bag, along with those rocks that together amounted to 23 pounds of raw, dead weight. They were meant to hold down the bag and ensure its secret did not surface.

It almost didn't.

A passerby first stumbled upon the blue-and-brown plaid canvas bag on April 21, 1970. It was what was known as a club bag, with a zipper on the top and handy pockets on the side—the the sort that might be used for a quick overnight trip. It could have even made a good diaper bag to carry all those essentials that come with new motherhood.

The bag in which the infant's body was found. Courtesy of the RCMP.

Instead, it carried a baby and two rocks.

That first passerby mistook the contents for the body of a dog. The man left the bag as he found it, on the ice of the South Saskatchewan River. It was below the bridge, at the south end, in Saskatchewan Landing Provincial Park.

And it was there that, two days later, a school bus broke down as it crossed the river that afternoon. The bus was carrying a group of high school students. The curiosity of two of the students, from Elrose, took them down to the river, to the east bank and to the abandoned bag on the ice.

The river had frozen over that December, so police investigators knew the bag must have been placed there sometime afterwards. But for the students' arrival sooner than spring thaw, the weighted bag with the baby's tiny body might have quietly slipped away.

It's unclear if the baby boy had lain sucking on his soother until slowly falling into a sleep from which he would never awake. Or perhaps he was already dead, the soother discarded along with the body, when placed in the bag.

At least one person probably knows for sure, but he or she has never surfaced, unlike the child's body.

Checks with high school counsellors and doctors and registrations for all live births in the province failed to turn up anything.

On April 8, 1970, some two weeks before the students' startling discovery, a car was seen parked near the bridge. It was a Buick or Oldsmobile, greenish-blue in colour, likely a model between 1967 and 1969. It may not have anything to do with the baby, or it might have everything to do with him. As with so much else, police simply don't have the answer because the owners have never been identified.

* * *

He, or perhaps she, was also found in the spring. But for a small hand reaching out from the stained towels, no one might have noticed.

The weathered shed was not the sort of building that would attract much attention. It was sturdy and serviceable to be sure—four sheets of plywood long and three wide with a metal roof—but not the type that would normally get a second thought. And perhaps that was its attraction.

By mid-afternoon on May 28, 1987, with the help of a tractor and a team of horses, the building had been urged from its old location in a yard south of Saskatoon to a new one about a hundred yards to the north. It was early evening before anyone returned to the original site for the task of cleanup. That's when the bundle of what looked like a discarded towel was spotted and opened to reveal the hand. When both towels in the bundle were pulled back, they showed the decomposed body of a newborn.

The body of the full-term infant had lain hidden between the railway ties beneath the shed for two or three years. It was shielded from predators, but not the ravages of time.

The shed under which the infant's body was found. Courtesy of the RCMP.

Whether boy or girl is as uncertain as how the body came to be there, but a pathologist felt certain the child was of aboriginal ancestry.

Investigators turned to hospitals, First Nation reserves, social workers, and forensic science in an effort to find out more—to no avail.

The two lives and deaths were unrelated, except for a shared fate. The bundles were small, the sort that might be missed, or dismissed. And they might have easily been both. But sometimes fate finds a way.

$320

It came out to $320, and that's all he wanted. Just *what he was owed*. What was *fair*. Just the money as they had agreed months ago, a fair wage for four and a half months' work in the sun and the bugs and the wind. Enough to get on a boat and go home to the old country before winter came.

But when John Kozi told his boss he wanted the wages he was owed, George Simon simply shrugged it off.

The trouble between them blew in on a big wind one Monday morning in September 1920, as George and John were working together on George's farm south of Viscount. With the gusting winds whipping the horse's reins back and forth between them, George yelled and swore, criticizing John and saying John wasn't strong enough to do the work.

"George, I am not your dog and I will not work for you any more," John finally told him. "Pay me my money, and I will go."

"You can go," George replied. "But I won't pay you a cent."

"I give you three days' time to make ready my wages," John said. "And then I go my way."

The next morning, John again approached his boss, who was preparing to leave for Saskatoon to find some new workers.

"I will not pay you," George said. "And you can go where it pleases you."

There were three new workers at the farm by Friday, and George was eating lunch with them when John walked into the house.

They had argued earlier that morning, exchanging hard, loud words in Hungarian, both men's mother tongue. Margaret Folz, who was cooking for the men, could hear George swearing as she made lunch.

When George called John to join him and the other men at the table now, John refused.

"No. The time is over," John said. "I am not going to dinner any more. I don't want your dinner."

As George got up and walked away from the table, John took a shell from his pocket and loaded it into the gun in his hand. This time, he called to his boss in English.

"Stop."

John fired one shot into George's back. George fell to the floor and lay there still.

"You have drove me crazy," said John.

John broke the gun apart on a stoneboat sitting beside the door, then put on his coat and started walking north, towards the closest police detachment.

"You are dead," he said, as he walked away. "And now I will die. The farmer will fool nobody no more."

* * *

John Kozi went on trial for murder in November. He spoke little English and barely understood the proceedings that would determine his life or death.

The Hungarian immigrant had been in Canada for several years, first working at a steel factory in Ontario, and then moving west as a farmhand and labourer. He never had any trouble until he started working for George Simon early in the summer of 1920.

George, however, had plenty of problems. Around Viscount, there were many stories about him, and some of them were recounted at John's trial.

There was the hired man who had worked with George three years earlier, slaved for months on the agreement of fair pay, but when his time was up George gave him only pennies of his due.

There were the Polish workers who took George to court twice for their pay, and there was the worker John Fish, whom George grabbed by the throat one day and tried to strangle during a fight over the plough.

One of John's former bosses, Steve Palti, spoke highly of John and said he'd heard many stories about George Simon refusing to pay his workers.

The jury deliberated for three hours before finding John Kozi guilty of murder. The jury made a strong recommendation for mercy.

Since the murder conviction came with an automatic death sentence, Justice Frederick Haultain added his own plea for leniency to the governor general, who would review the case.

"Evidence in black and white does not look favourable, but Kozi is an uneducated foreigner who does not speak English...," Haultain wrote. "Further enquiries have confirmed my opinion that crime was result of ill-treatment and threatened loss of whole season's wages under aggravated circumstances and was committed in heat of passion roused in last violent quarrel."

Haultain said his "very strong impression" in favour of the worker John Kozi—and his feelings against the employer George Simon—had been made even stronger by looking further into the case outside the court proceedings.

Over two thousand others lent their names to a petition begging for mercy on John's behalf. In the face of such strong opposition, the death sentence that had been set for January 26, 1921, was commuted to a term of life imprisonment.

But Kozi spent only three months in prison before facing a different sentence. His fate was marked in a brief notation on his prison file in April 1921, almost one year after he first began working for George Simon.

"This is to advise you that inmate John Kozi, No. 634 of Saskatchewan Penitentiary was removed to the Asylum for the Insane at Battleford, Saskatchewan."

DEVIL'S TOOLS

They lived in the limbo better known as remand—the time and space between arrest and, quite often, conviction. An array of accused thugs, robbers, misfits, and killers, they were doing dead time.

The plan was hatched more from boredom than desperation. None of them really believed it would work. But it engaged hands and minds, giving them a purpose that they often lacked on the outside. They knew the inside well, sort of like having a home you could always go back to but without a house key. They had been coming here, or places like here, since they were teenage boys. On the inside of those aging walls with the chipped paint, cracks, and graffitied artwork were friends and family and guys from the neighbourhood who had different names but the same life.

Most of them had nothing to lose, really. This was unit 3A, a motley band of 17 high-security inmates: Nine charged with murder, two with attempted murder, and six with other serious crimes. All of those divided between the 14 cells had ties to street gangs.

Their cellblock at the Regina Provincial Correctional Centre had been built in 1964, when *The Great Escape* was in the running for an Academy Award, and a hacksaw from the Army and Navy Department Store in downtown Regina cost 88¢. None of the guys who would execute the plan to get outside those bars had been born when they were installed. Most were in the 20s; the oldest 32.

The interior side walls were made of cinder blocks—each eight inches by six inches and four inches thick—with fine metal rods inside. Red brick covered the outside walls. The four decades that had passed since construction had taken a toll. After an escape in 2004 revealed that the mortar around the blocks could be easily removed, the upper portion above the heating registers was covered with sheet metal.

The inmates started by picking up things that might come in handy—broom handles, tiles, scraps of metal, a hacksaw blade foraged from the maintenance tunnels, a cutlery holder, and bed linens. Someone discovered the towel bar cut off a desk could come in handy for prying and scraping. The real work got under way in May 2008.

The guys moved a table into the end of the long corridor and sat there most days and nights playing cards until lock-up. At least, to the guards, that's what it looked like they were doing. The inmates put on their best poker faces and took a gamble. Luckily, the security camera at that end of the corridor had a significant blind spot—so did the guards, as it turned out.

Behind the facade of the cards, inmates were waging their own high-stakes game. The card players or the other inmates who stood in the corridor exercising blocked the camera's view of those moving the grille on and off the heating vent. A rejigged nail clipper proved handy to remove and replace the screws. Then it was a matter of cutting and tearing through the steel plate lining the back of the heat register to get to the brick wall. That took more than a month alone. Once they got through it though, they hit the cinder blocks and chipped away at the aging mortar between them. They carried the dust and debris from their slow but steady progress on their clothes. Still, no one noticed, even when they flushed the rubble into the sewer system.

Once they were through the cinder, only the red bricks remained. Red—it had to seem like a lucky colour for the gang members who had made it their trademark.

They expected to get caught at almost every turn. One guard had even heard something, back at the end of June.

Word on the street was that some inmates were "going to be out soon" and "they are doing it like the movies." But when nothing of the sort had happened by early July, it was chalked up to old news.

After another tip about a possible escape, the cells and the inmates got shaken down on July 9 for weapons, drugs, and anything else that wasn't supposed to be there. The would-be escapees thought their scheme was likely over. The unit was put on lockdown—total confinement. The inmates' drab grey sweatpants and shirts were replaced by yellow, the mark of a secure range.

After two weeks, they were back to grey. But only half the guys could be out of their cells for half the day; the rest got the other half. It blew over though, and they were back on track.

They tried to think of everything—a piece of canvas torn from a jail-issue winter jacket to position behind the grate and cover progress on the hole; sheets and scraps of cloth braided into ropes; and green jail-issue parkas to cover the razor wire on the perimeter fence.

Four months passed, and 87 different guards came and went—and still no one was the wiser. Maybe we really can pull this off, the inmates thought. They had to make their move before the jail administration did. The new remand building was almost complete, and soon they would be relocated. Then all the work would be for naught.

They picked their night: A breezy but warm Sunday, August 24, 2008.

A guard took a count of the inmates at 8:30 that evening. Five minutes later, the escapees removed the cover from the heating vent and smashed through the weakened red brick wall with a shower rod. First out was Daniel, the agile inmate balancing on a narrow ledge, three metres off the ground. Another escapee handed him the homemade rope, fashioned from braided blankets and bedsheets with a metal bar on the end. Daniel tossed it over the adjacent wall and signalled to the rest. His half-brother and four more inmates emerged from the hole. Each in turn scaled the compound wall, laying winter coats across the top to protect them from the rolls of razor wire. Once over the top, they shimmied down the rope and dropped to the ground in the exercise yard. In similar fashion, they scaled two more barbed-wire fences to complete their escape.

Adrenalin pulsing through their bodies, the ex-inmates hit the ground, scattered—and kept on running.

A full hour and five minutes passed before there was any hint of their absence.

A call from Regina police, tipped off to a possible escape attempt, had guards quickly heading for Unit 3A. The make-shift ropes dangling from the compound wall told them the possibility was a gut-wrenching reality.

Chaos broke out on 3A. The remaining inmates smashed windows. A sink, ripped from a cell wall, blocked the corridor—to slow down the guards and buy time for the escapees. The guards entered with shields and batons.

With the inmates masking their faces, it took some time to sort out who was there—and who wasn't. Gone from Cell 2 were Preston Clarence Buffalocalf and Cody Dillon Keenatch. Buffalocalf was awaiting trial for a shooting that left a man dead. Gone from Cell 3 was Ryan Joseph Agecoutay, sitting on remand for more than a year after a vicious attack that left a man near death in an alley. In Agecoutay's place, police found a dummy covered with a blanket. Likewise, Kenneth Leigh Iron was gone from Cell 7. He was facing trial for twice driving over a man. "Next time, I'll fucking kill him," Iron had menaced after breaking his victim's pelvis. James Joseph Pewean, accused of murder and attempted murder, was also AWOL from Cell 6.

They were all dangerous men, but it was Pewean's absent cellmate who caused the most anxiety among his former captors and the police. Accused of shooting two people to death and leaving three more clinging to life, Daniel Richard Wolfe, Buffalocalf's half-brother, had mused after his arrest about taking out some witnesses if he ever got the chance.

And now he was free.

* * *

Iron was the first one caught. He hadn't even made it very far when police found him two hours later by a hockey rink.

The others would find fleeting freedom for days and even weeks longer. But within a month, they were all back where they started, behind bars. For Wolfe, the ending was a lot like the beginning. He was picked up on the streets of Winnipeg, where he had started his life of crime breaking into instead of out of places before graduating to robbery and ultimately multiple murder. Fifteen months after the escape, he received a life sentence.

A censored report, released publicly, about how six dangerous inmates chipping away for four months in a bid for freedom had escaped the notice of 87 guards contained almost as many holes as the crumbling jail. But there was one very candid observation: "The statement, 'Idle hands are the devil's tools' has strong application at the [Regina Provincial Correctional Centre] in the remand and segregated areas … When people have large blocks of time on their hands with nothing constructive to do, they tend to gravitate towards doing whatever they can get away with."

When he sentenced Agecoutay, the last of the escapees, Justice Maurice Herauf pondered their efforts and the wasted potential. "It was quite a feat," he said. "If the people that were involved in that used a bit of their time to improve their life, they might be model citizens in the future."

Agecoutay stood in court that day wearing a T-shirt that seemed silently to mock the judge's prediction. It read, or rather boasted, Thug Life.

Thirteen months later, Agecoutay was one of six prisoners accused of helping to kill a man, stabbed once in the chest while trying to intervene in a brawl that left the two intended targets bleeding but alive.

Daniel Wolfe finally escaped his life sentence at age 33, a dead man.

THE LAST STRAW

The fire had easily eaten through almost the entire hay-stack, except the bits around the edges where the snow still covered the straw. Neighbours had noticed the blaze on the morning of April 11, 1933, but several days passed before Mike Swyck went for a closer look. His dog was sniffing at the remnants when he drew his master's attention to something in the ashes. Swyck initially took it for a soup bone, at least until he picked it up. Turning the mass over in his hands, Swyck recognized what he held wasn't what he had thought. It was, in fact, a skull. And there were more charred remains. Something shiny also poked out from among the black ash. The brass buckle from a pair of overalls was still recognizable, even if the wearer wasn't.

RCMP officers summoned to the farm in the Whitkow district found more—two cufflinks, a collar button, two more overall buckles, four fasteners, boot eyelets, barbed wire, and three steel buttons stamped "Loss Proof" on their faces. The pile of ashes was almost two feet deep in the centre. That's where they discovered the body parts—more pieces of skull, pelvic bones, an upper thigh, several teeth, and what looked like charred flesh. Three copper jackets from bullets added to the mystery.

Attempts to put a name to the nearly destroyed remains were futile. But pathologist Dr. Frances McGill felt certain the deceased was a short, fat man, judging by the bones that were recovered.

Investigators were skeptical. They had been searching for Nestor Tereszczuk since the fall of 1932. He was short and thin—and the police suspected it might have been him in the haystack. One family in the district had plenty of reason to want Tereszczuk gone. He had married Annie Bahrey in 1931. But then the family found out Tereszczuk was already married, to a woman back in Poland. That made him a bigamist, his marriage to Annie a sham. And that didn't sit well with some of the Bahreys, a large family of eight siblings.

Annie's brother Alex Bahrey had suspiciously disappeared from the district a day before residents in the area spied the burning haystack. Alex was often in trouble—and some of it had landed him in jail. Usually it was for theft. His last stint, in 1925, was for a year of hard labour after stealing a bookcase, a couple of armchairs, a clock, and two lamps from the school – taken during a heavy snowstorm. A provincial police magistrate, urging that Alex not get parole, said he was known as a "big nuisance" in the Whitkow district, an area of mostly Ukrainian homesteaders about 40 miles northeast of North Battleford. The police didn't hold out much hope Alex would change once released.

His wife, Dora, believed Alex was going out to trap muskrats when he left their farm with his horse on April 10. She still hadn't seen him more than a week later.

And, privately at least, the 25-year-old woman was just as glad.

Alex was not an easy man to live with, and his temper fuelled a lot of arguments. Usually the rows left Dora bloodied and crying. No one had ever hit her before she married Alex in February 1931. Shortly after their wedding, Alex had threatened to bury her alive if she told the police about his homebrew or his wheat stealing. More than once he had threatened to kill her. "I'll tear you in two pieces and tie a rock to your neck and drown you," she remembered him saying. Three weeks after their baby was born, Alex had left, forcing Dora to tread through deep snow in the terrible cold in order to get wood to light a fire in their one-bedroom shack.

Fifteen days after Alex had left to go hunting, his sorrel mare was found tied to a tree. The horse was identified by Alex's brother Bill Bahrey.

Only two years apart in age, Bill and his older brother Alex couldn't be more different. To their father, Ambrose, Bill was "a good boy," even-tempered, mild-mannered. Alex was his troubled wild child, who had spent time in an asylum. Bill was a hard worker; Alex was most decidedly not. Just that fall, Bill had accused Alex of stealing his wheat. The brothers home-steaded adjoining quarter sections, and Bill often stayed with Alex and Dora.

Questioned by police, Bill revealed that the remains in the straw stack were those of his brother-in-law Nestor Tereszczuk. Nestor had come to Alex's house, and the two men had left together. But an hour later, Alex returned with blood on his hands, his cap, his coat, and his face. When Bill asked about it, Alex told him he had fallen off his horse. Then Alex left that night, saying only that he was going north.

Later, Bill gave another statement, confessing that he and Alex had together killed Nestor. Alex took Nestor to the top of the straw pile, and Bill fired at him as Nestor tried to get away. Finally, with Alex firmly holding onto his brother-in-law, Bill fired three more times—in the chest, the left eye, and the top of the head. The next day, Bill went back and set the straw on fire. Alex left on horseback.

Ambrose had heard his son testify at the coroner's inquest that the body in the straw stack was Nestor. But Ambrose didn't believe him. At the urging of his father to tell the truth, Bill gave police his final statement.

In November 1932, Bill had shot his former brother-in-law in the breast as he walked from the house to the barn. The shot, however, didn't kill him, so Bill clubbed Nestor with the hub of a broken wheel. Bill tied a logging chain to Nestor's feet that night and dragged him by horse to a straw pile, then set it on fire.

But it wasn't the same straw pile where Swyck's dog had discovered the remains of what the pathologist insisted was a short, "thick set" man.

Alex Bahrey was about five-foot-six and weighed almost 170 pounds.

The two brothers were alone at Alex's home when Dora and Annie went April 9 to visit Ambrose Bahrey for a few days. The next day, Alex left to get beer bottles from Mike Swyck. Alex was hiding the bottles in the straw stack when Bill, lying in wait between a granary and a snowdrift, lifted his rifle and fired once at his brother. He missed his target. So Bill moved to the top of the stack and fired three more times down upon his brother. He hid the body in the straw. Returning to the stack at daybreak the next day, Bill tied barbed wire around Alex's arm and pulled his brother's body on top of the stack. Bill set it aflame.

He left Alex's sorrel mare tied up in the bluff so people would think his brother had run away. He tossed the rifle in the creek and hid the shells in his father's barn under the manger.

When Dora returned from visiting at her father-in-law's home on April 12, Bill told her Alex had gone hunting muskrats. But a couple of days later, when she found her husband's mackinaw coat and his watch hidden in the barn, she demanded an explanation from Bill. She knew what he had done to Nestor; the whole family did. She asked if her husband had met the same fate. "Yes, and you keep quiet," he said. He warned her that if she didn't keep it to herself, she might meet the same fate.

Bill didn't like the way Nestor and Alex treated the women, so he set out to stop it. He liked Dora. He particularly liked those times he had shared her bed. (Dora would tell the court Alex had sent Bill to her.) Two years earlier, when Alex had beaten her so badly she wanted to go to the police, Bill had talked her out of it, saying he would kill Alex.

A doctor from the mental hospital at Battleford was called as a witness for the defence to determine if Bill was fit

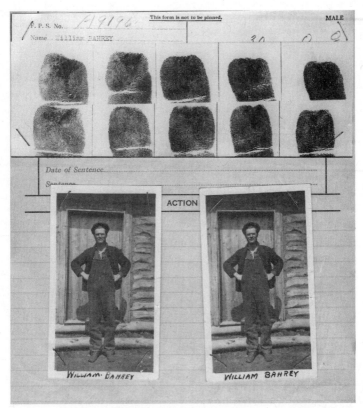

Bill Bahrey, 1925–1934. Copyright Government of Canada. Reproduced with the permission of the Minister of Public Works and Government Services Canada (2007). Source: Library and Archives Canada/Department of Justice fonds/RG 13-B-1/File no. cc 402.

to stand trial. While Bill physically was a man of 27, the doctor said he was mentally a boy of eight to ten years. Still, the accused knew the difference between right and wrong. Bill was pronounced fit to stand trial for murdering his brother.

The defence suggested Bill was the scapegoat, a simpleton sent by his family to commit murder.

It took the jury a mere 10 minutes to find Bill guilty of fratricide. It was his first—and last—criminal conviction. The Crown never bothered to run the trial for Nestor's death.

Bill Bahrey was hanged from a scaffold in Prince Albert on February 23, 1934.

A BUDDING CAREER

He started out quite small, in the low-rent district of the Criminal Code. It was not the sort of thing that attracts much notice or demands headlines. The charge was "false pretences"—knowingly holding out something false, usually a bogus cheque, with the intention that the victim will act on it. An almost-imperceptible blip in the annals of crime, the offence drew one year's probation and an order to repay the $211.71 swindled from the victim.

Case closed.

The seed was planted that day, March 7, 1979, in a Saskatoon courtroom. That's when Gordon Karl Summers, at age 22, recorded his first adult criminal conviction. He received a conditional discharge. It meant that if he kept out of trouble for a year and paid back the ill-gotten money, he could walk away without a criminal record. The seed would never take root.

But Gordon was back in court for sentencing five months later for false pretences and fraud. This time, his probation order came with a three-month jail sentence. And he had to repay $128.66.

The next time it was a Prince Albert courtroom, where he added convictions for more of the same. Gordon had gained a firm foothold in the criminal courts in half a year. Like a weed on the prairies, once the roots take hold, a budding con can flourish given the right conditions.

Gordon proved persistent and vigorous, a thistle in the side of the justice system. His record grew under the weight of more frauds and false pretences, as did the penalties. By 1986, he had traded in jail terms for a prison cell.

In the past, Gordon had thought small—petty cheques and dine-and-dashes. It was time to adapt and branch out. The 1990s were ripe for a grander vision, one that included an oil exploration business and a school to teach students about heavy-duty equipment. Somewhat familiar with Manitoba (having served time in Stony Mountain Penitentiary), the Saskatchewan transplant residing in Edmonton planned to open up shop in Churchill. Gordon and his business partner began cultivating their idea in the northern Manitoba community in the spring of 1994. By summer, the plan had withered under the heat.

That heat came from Edmonton police officers, who waged a two-month-long investigation. Gordon and his partner landed in jail after a raid turned up a raft of stolen property, including equipment capable of churning out phony driver's licences, validation tags, and insurance forms—perhaps a means of finding some seed money for their Manitoba enterprise. The fake licences were pretty good, since they were produced using cameras, laminators, and other equipment stolen from official motor vehicle branch offices in rural Alberta. While the counterfeit IDs looked real, the bogus bombs were better. Even the experts were fooled by the car alarms attached to plasticine—not plastic explosives. They surfaced in the search that also yielded a booklet, intended for bank staff, on what to do in the event of a robbery, along with a note threatening that a bomb would be detonated by remote control.

Gordon was ready to make a new start after he got out of jail for that caper. He hit pay dirt in North Bay, Ontario. It took three years for investigators to unravel his schemes. He settled into the Cozy Camp Cottages on picturesque Lake Nosbonsing in 1997. Founder of Titania Oil and Gas Canada Incorporated, Summers had a plan to extract and process crude oil and natural gas on the Hudson Bay basin. The offices of Titania pumped out news releases about out-of-province deals, expansion plans, and dreams for a line of gas stations that would undercut the competitors.

A public offering was in the offing, with Titania shares expected to go for 20¢ apiece. Listed on the Toronto Stock Exchange, Titania investments would yield eight-percent returns quarterly, and a considerable tax credit. The $10-million refinery would create two hundred jobs. At least that's what Gordon told anyone who would listen. Some 160 people bought in—and Gordon cashed out, draining investors of $434,900 with his lies.

But Gordon hadn't completely made a break with his past, falling back on the mainstays of his criminal career. At the same time he was bilking Titania investors, he cashed two bogus cheques, including one for $28,000 stolen from a real businessman. Summers already had the cash in hand before the bank discovered the forgery.

It was the fall of 2000 when Gordon found himself back in familiar territory, the prisoner's dock. Having already spent 11 months behind bars on this occasion, Summers received a further 27-month prison sentence in the North Bay courtroom.

Freed in February 2003, he was passing bad cheques by the summer of the next year. If Titania had taught Gordon anything, it was that he needn't think small. Summers surfaced in Kenora, Ontario, in the spring of 2005, sprouting a new idea. He was looking for investors for a 10,000-square-foot biotechnology manufacturing facility—a $2-million initiative promising more than a hundred jobs. Vigor Biotics would manufacture the cancer-fighting drug paclitaxel, extracting it from the leaves of Canadian yew plants. Gordon told *Northern Ontario Business* magazine he had land leased, backing from a significant New Brunswick investor's fund, a Quebec seller, and suppliers from Saskatchewan to China. "In five years' time I hope some big pharmaceutical manufacturer will buy us out," Summers mused while telling journalist Kelly Louiseize about the plant.

Much like seeds, ideas can't grow without a certain amount of manure. No one contacted by the magazine backed up Gordon's claims.

Still, by the fall of that year, Gordon had inked an agreement with an American businessman. He didn't hear much from Summers for the next few months. He was told Gordon was away on business or out checking fields. What he didn't know was that Gordon was behind bars, serving the 11-month sentence for forged cheques passed a year earlier.

Summers lost no time after his release in July 2006. Believing there was still money to be made in yew extract, despite the bad press, the undaunted, resilient, wannabe businessman set out for greener pastures. He found them in Hanley, Saskatchewan, about a half hour south of Saskatoon, where Gordon had his start.

Tired of the hustle and bustle of a big city, and finding a lack of industrial space in Kenora, he looked further west to find a base for his new operation, Vigor Biopharma, he said. He was particularly attracted, he told the *StarPhoenix* newspaper, by the "ease of doing business in Saskatchewan.

"We're coming home," he said.

The town was buzzing with Gordon's plans for a 30,000-square-foot yew extraction facility that would reap $2.5 million in annual revenue and bring 80 jobs to the small town. A summary financial statement for Vigor listed total assets of $149 million, and a gross profit of $4.2 million. The roots of Gordon's scheme reached all the way to China.

Impressed by Vigor's financials, British Columbia-based Sino Pharmaceuticals filled Summers' order for $245,000 US worth of paclitaxel. Five kilograms of the anti-cancer drug arrived from China in April 2007. Two California investors, also impressed by Vigor's promising projections, ponied up $30,764 to pay for shipping.

Over the years, as his schemes grew, Summers convinced people he was a doctor, a scientist, a geologist, and a bio-technologist. He was none of those things. He had some training in accounting from a technical school—and a fertile imagination.

In the spring of 2009, Gordon Karl Summers (also known as Gordon Seeman and Gordon Siemens) was back in a Saskatoon courtroom. That seed planted three decades earlier had grown considerably. His record stretched to 54 convictions, the bulk of them for fraud offences, and on this day in April, he was to be sentenced for two more: Defrauding Sino Pharmaceuticals and the California investors of a grand total of $275,764.

The man whose first crime had gone virtually unnoticed left a significant mark with his 55th and 56th offences. Having lost the drug and its money, Sino Pharmaceuticals had to hold off on plans to grow the company. The China-based manager who had entered the deal with Summers had a nervous breakdown.

"It certainly shatters one's idealism," wrote the president of the company.

Unable to nip Summers in the bud 30 years earlier, the courts would try again in hopes a three-year prison sentence would convince him to turn over a new leaf.

SUSPICION

Mary always had the axe with her when she went out to cut wood on the road allowance. She had made the handle herself, fashioning it from a piece of willow. Peter Lasch was on his way to town, Jedburgh, to pick up his mail when he passed Mary around noon that day. No one could fault the elderly woman for her work ethic or her frugality. She was pulling up brush and stacking it along the side of the road. One of the farmers in the area had promised to haul it for her when he found some time. Winter's chill was already in the air, and Mary would need the firewood.

The 65-year-old widow was quite a sight that afternoon. She was dressed in every stitch of clothing she owned. She wore a pink blouse and two dresses—a plaid one on the outside and a polka-dot one covering her cotton undershirt. They were tucked into a pair of overalls, and a stocking was tied around her middle. Mary had wrapped twine around each of her pant legs, which disappeared into her rubber boots. The layers were topped off with a ragged overcoat. Her hands were in mittens, while a babushka covered her greying dark-brown hair, which was pulled back into a bun. Over the head scarf was a fur cap, the earflaps pulled down and the strap fastened beneath her chin.

Mary had grown accustomed to hard work. She had come from the old country in March 1910, married a short time later, and worked alongside her husband as a homesteader. They didn't have any children. She had been on her own for almost 20 years now since her husband, Michael, had died. In recent years, she had bounced between the homes of relatives or stayed at neighbouring farms where she found work.

Mary had lived on and off for the past four years in a small shack built by her brother Mike Dobko near his own house. Sometimes she would disappear for several days at a stretch. Usually, no one thought too much about her absences. Mary would occasionally find work in the area and stay with her employer until the job was completed, like when she worked for Urbanowski picking stones for a dollar a day. In the summer months, she picked Seneca root and sold it to the store in nearby Willowbrook. She preferred to be paid in dollar bills since she had trouble telling the $20 bills apart from the ones—and she didn't want to chance getting them confused.

Over the years, the thrifty senior had managed to tuck away quite a few dollars. No one knew exactly how much money she had amassed, but friends and family suspected it was far more than many of them had. From time to time, they turned to Mary when they ran short. Only that spring, her sister-in-law had borrowed money to buy a cream separator. Mary had handed her $50 dollars, digging it out from somewhere inside her vest. The sister-in-law gave her the $15 dollars in change back a month later, after her purchase, but never did repay the rest. Sometimes she gave Mary milk, bread, and other food, so the sister-in-law figured the money was due. It wasn't the first time one of Mary's loans went unpaid. A neighbour had borrowed $200 from her back in 1932—then failed to pay back any of it. But Mary hired a lawyer and eventually collected the debt. Once, several years earlier, when she had loaned a different neighbour $80, he noticed that often she carried her cash with her. He had advised her then to put it in a bank.

It was around noon on November 13, 1937, when people in the area saw Mary working with her axe along the roadside.

Almost a year would pass before anyone saw her again.

A hole in amongst the scrub brush caught Bill Panio's interest as he picked mushrooms in the Beaver Hills Forest

Reserve. He thought the depression looked like something an animal might have dug—until he noticed a pair of women's stockings poking out from the overturned soil. Then Bill saw a bone that jutted up from sunken ground.

After running home to tell his parents, Bill returned with his father. Demko Panio pushed his garden fork into the disturbed earth. About four inches down, he hit what felt like clothing. Demko pushed aside some unearthed rags to reveal yellowed, dead grass, like the kind one sees in the fall. It was at odds with the green hues of this summer day on July 17, 1938.

But then, so was the human head, which was their next discovery.

The police officers arrived the next morning.

Corporal C. H. Harvey followed Demko Panio to the spot, about 70 feet into the bush from a clearing. A thigh bone was sticking out from the ground. The makeshift grave was shallow, likely not more than 18 inches deep when it was first dug. The earth had collapsed over the winter and spring. Pushed into a grave too small for its four-foot-eleven frame, the corpse was lying on its back, turned slightly to the left with the knees drawn up to the torso in a two-by-four-foot space. Time and scavengers had taken their toll. While the face was unrecognizable, the clothes were unmistakable—the black cap still fastened by a button, the layers of dresses and shirts, the old, patched black-and-white striped coveralls, and the green overcoat that had been tossed over the remains.

This was Mary Wagera.

During the autopsy, investigators found $1.52 in coins wrapped in a cotton handkerchief and hidden in the pocket of her undershirt.

Her corpse also carried another secret—the means of her death. Mary had suffered two blows, maybe even three, to her head from a heavy blunt object. She had likely drawn a few breaths after she was struck, but certainly not many given the severe skull fracture. A pathologist believed the object that had caused such damage was quite possibly the blunt end of an axe, like the one Mary was using the last day area residents saw her alive.

Who would want Mary dead?

RCMP investigators couldn't answer that question, but they felt confident they knew why she was killed. According to one woman, Mary had once said she had saved upwards of $700.

Police had plenty of suspicions about that missing cash. People who were formerly on relief in the area were suddenly spending money fairly freely. Investigators wondered about a large property purchase made six months after Mary disappeared. It was paid for with a lot of smaller denomination bills, like the ones Mary favoured when she sold her Seneca roots. And much of the money was the older, larger-sized bills that had been out of circulation since 1935.

Those suspicions deepened when a Repeater Tobacco tin box surfaced at one home in the area. Forensic testing showed that the bottom of the box had traces of cobbler's wax and tar—just like the box Mary used to have in which she kept an awl, wax, shoe tacks, and needles—and quite possibly her cash.

The box also contained an older-style large dollar bill, two smaller dollar bills, and shinplasters or paper 25¢ bills. One neighbour had told police how Mary had worked for him about five years ago, helping him plaster the chicken house. He had paid her with a shinplaster that had been kept for a considerable length of time in a billfold. The man recognized the shinplaster by the way it was folded, and lab tests found it carried traces of a substance similar to that of the billfold.

Police asked a lot of questions—and they got answers. But the contradictions in people's stories seemed to pile up like cordwood. Police were convinced Mary was the victim of a premeditated murder, lured away by a killer intent on stealing her money.

The investigation was a bit like putting together a puzzle, except without having a picture to follow or knowing how many pieces there were—let alone how they fit together.

Police thought they were getting closer to a solution in June 1939 when a farmer spotted something as his horse pulled harrows across a ravine. That something was an axe, probably Mary's. A small area around it had been burned, feeding suspicions that someone had been trying to destroy evidence.

Over the days and months and years after Mary and what was likely her axe were found, police tried to solve that puzzle. But the picture was always incomplete.

At least three prosecutors hired by the attorney general's office reviewed the evidence. There were as many layers to the circumstantial case as Mary's clothes. "Past experience has taught peace officers that when a suspect goes out of his way to create alibis or change his previous statements, it is because he has good reasons to cover up his connection with the crime concerned," read one report. "This is exactly the situation that we find in this particular investigation."

The attorney general's office directed the RCMP in April 1943 to consider the file closed. There was suspicion—strong suspicion—but only that.

BOILING POINT

Peering through the coach window, the dark-haired man on the train took in the prairie landscape. A faint smile played on his lips. At Carmel, the first stop on his journey, a large crowd had gathered on the platform. It had been the same at Humboldt, where people had filled the depot to see off the Polish immigrant who had once worked on this railroad as a section hand. Settled in his seat, he smoked a cigarette, seemingly oblivious to the crowds, except for a wave to one of his friends. A journalist, working hard to keep his typewriter balanced with the jostling of the train, recorded every move of the infamous traveller. The reporter took note as the man turned to his seatmate and commented how he might yet return to Humboldt one day.

"Three months is a long time," he told his guard.

The 28-year-old man, his hands manacled, was on his way to his death. On June 30, 1930, he had an appointment with hangman Arthur Ellis on the scaffold at the Prince Albert prison.

* * *

Antena Kropa and Alexander Wysochan lay next to one another on the bedroom floor this Christmas night. Her neck rested on his right arm, and one of her legs was twisted across one of Alex's.

Between them on the floor, about chest level, lay a revolver.

Alex had a wound roughly the size of a 50-cent piece on his left side. His pulse was near normal, though he seemed dazed.

Remarkably, Antena was still breathing, despite the three bullets that left holes in her abdomen, her right hip, and her chest just beneath her breast. The bullet in her chest had ricocheted like a pinball, bouncing off her ribs, heading for her lungs, retreating to penetrate her diaphragm, then moving upwards to tear through her heart.

Finding the door to the house locked, police officers peered through a broken window to see Alex and Antena stretched out on the floor. Humboldt police Chief Denis Palmer and RCMP Sergeant Fred Evans crawled in through the window.

Dr. Harry Fleming bandaged Antena's wounds and ordered that she immediately be taken to hospital. The injured woman was mumbling words in Polish, but neither the doctor nor the two police officers nearby knew what she was saying or to whom. Both her husband, Stanley Kropa, and his friend Tony Sokolowski, who had opened the door seconds after police crawled in through the window, were nearby. According to Stanley, his wife called for him, stretching out her arms and pleading, "Stanley, help me, the bullet is right in me."

Neighbours moved Antena from the house—the same home she had tried to turn her back on days earlier—and put her on a sleigh that would carry her to the hospital. As Philip Mykolak, who lived across the street, pulled a blanket up over her, he heard Antena plead in Polish, "Stanley. Help. I am too hot."

Antena made it to the hospital, but within minutes the 25-year-old was dead.

Only then did Dr. Fleming turn his full attention to Alex. An x-ray revealed that the bullet, fired from a faulty gun, had not penetrated his body. It dropped from his thick jacket during the examination. Still, the bullet had left a mark about three inches above Alex's left nipple. Fleming could smell the booze on his patient, and felt that it, rather than the bullet, was the more likely explanation for the patient's confused state. In the morning, after Alex had a chance to sleep off some of the alcohol's effects, Fleming asked him who was responsible.

Alex didn't really answer except to say, "I suppose a rope will be put around my neck."

Fleming repeated his question. "I didn't do it," Alex replied.

Alex and Antena first met in November 1929 when they had each gone separately to the locomotive foreman for hot water. Antena didn't have any mittens, so Alex offered to carry the boiling water back to her house. He went there a good many more times afterwards, often when her husband was absent.

Stanley was home on December 11 when Alex came over. The trio played cards and shared a jug of red wine. After a while, Stanley didn't feel so good. Antena pulled off his boots, and Stanley fell asleep. He awoke around 3:00 a.m. to find himself alone. Not only was Antena gone, but so were her clothes.

Stanley sought help from the Humboldt police. He and Chief Palmer knocked on the door of room 3 at the Royal Café later that evening. When there wasn't an immediate answer, they walked in to find Alex sprawled across the foot of the unmade bed. He and Antena were fully clothed, but Alex was buttoning up the fly of his pants as he walked out from behind the bed.

Palmer asked if the room belonged to Alex, and when Alex said no, the police chief strongly suggested that he stay away from there. Meanwhile, Stanley, speaking in Polish, pleaded with his wife—the woman he had married nearly six years earlier in the old country and the mother of their three-and-a-half-year-old son. But Antena pushed away from his embrace, laughing at her husband. Realizing he wasn't getting anywhere, Stanley grabbed her valise and a bundle of clothing and left as Antena and Alex went downstairs for dinner.

Palmer and Stanley, as well as Mayor J. G. Crawley and Philip Mykolyk, to act as interpreter, went to Alex's shack the next day to try again to fix the mess. "I did everything I could to get that woman to go home to her child and to her husband," Chief Palmer would recall. Stanley tried once more to embrace his wife. Again, she laughed at him.

Palmer didn't want this kind of trouble in his town. He called Alex aside, grabbed him by the collar, and tried to talk some sense into him. "What are you going to do?" asked the police chief. "Are you going to let that woman go home to her child?"

Antena, fearful for Stanley because of the heavy-handed officer, finally relented. She went home.

Christmas Day found Antena's husband and her lover drinking beer at separate tables in the Arlington Hotel. Seated with Alex, Tony Sokolowski called Stanley over to join them. But Stanley didn't want anything to do with the man who had taken away his wife.

Stanley had gone to the bar to look for Tony and to get a key for the house. Antena and Stanley shared the house with Tony. But Tony retrieved the key from Alex—perhaps a gift from his lover. Stanley would later swear he knew nothing of Alex giving Tony the key.

As Stanley left the bar, Alex called to him.

"Go to hell," Stanley replied.

The two men ended up at the house several hours later. According to Alex, Stanley had asked Alex to follow him back to the house, where he found Antena in tears. He said Stanley tossed him up against a wall and said, "You won't run away with her any more." Alex said Antena was trying to pull Stanley off him when he heard the shots.

But by Stanley's account, Alex showed up uninvited and began threatening him and Antena at gunpoint in their bedroom, telling Antena, "Step back because I am going to kill him like a dog." Stanley jumped out the bedroom window, hearing four shots as he fled to the Mykolaks' house.

One passerby, who heard the gunshots and breaking glass, thought he saw a small boy running away. Looking inside, the passerby saw Antena with her hands out and Alex falling to the floor.

None of the shots had come from more than six to nine inches away.

There wasn't any question it was Alex's revolver. He had traded a .22-calibre rifle plus $1.90 for the rusty old handgun in September. But, according to Alex, the gun was in the valise that Stanley had taken from room 3. The valise held further evidence of the lovers' tryst, a photograph of Antena leaning into Alex, her arm resting on his legs as they stared at the camera. It had been taken in a Humboldt studio the week they met. Someone thought they'd seen the gun in Alex's pocket when they played rummy about a week before the shooting, but Alex denied it.

It seemed an open-and-shut case—a jealous husband, his dead wife, her wounded lover.

But it was Alex Wysochan who went on trial, defended by a rising star in the legal and political community named John G. Diefenbaker. The lawyer hired his own interpreter for the trial. And, more than a few times, Diefenbaker took issue with the Crown's translator.

The prosecutor and the judge suspected Wysochan's English was a lot better than he let on. "You started making love to this woman the first time you saw her?" began the cross-examination of Alex, who waited for the translation. "Never mind the interpreter. You know what I mean by making love. You got friendly with Antena Kropa the first time you saw her, didn't you?"

The interpreter told the court Alex was indicating he didn't understand.

"You go and sit down for a little while and see if we cannot get along without you," Justice Henry Bigelow told the interpreter. But when Alex repeatedly replied that he didn't understand the next series of questions, the interpreter was finally recalled.

When Alex told his version of being wounded by the revolver fired by Stanley, Diefenbaker asked him to show the jury his wound. "Have you a magnifying glass so we can see it?" the judge scoffed.

The jury believed the version of the thwarted adulterer bent on revenge (and described as a cowardly "reptile" by the prosecution) rather than the cuckolded husband out for blood. Within hours of his conviction, Alex was put on the train to the prison in Prince Albert. During his journey, he told a reporter about his life in Poland—his service in the Russian army fighting Bolshevists, his wife, his three step-children, his 81-year-old father and six brothers in a small town near Warsaw. It was where he'd been an altar boy in the church, and where his father played the organ.

Now, Alex prayed for his life.

The scaffold at the prison had sat idle for seven years. It had been built to hang Katarina Tracz, a woman convicted in the poisoning death of her husband, but there wasn't much appetite for hanging a woman. Her sentence was commuted to life, as were those of the condemned prisoners who followed—and Alex hoped he too might be spared.

The appeal court judges and the government thought otherwise. Alex kept his date with the hangman. Before mounting the scaffold, he met with a priest.

"I am innocent," said the condemned man in his broken English. "I did not kill anybody, but if God wants me, he can have me."

The letter, postmarked Zyrawa, Poland, arrived almost five years later, on April 6, 1935. Alex's wife, Melania, wanted compensation from the Canadian government.

"My husband … has been condemned to death by the Canadian court and the sentence was executed on him," read the English translation. "Recently, it has been revealed that my husband died shamefully as an innocent man."

The Justice Department turned her down in a letter of reply a month later. "I have the honour to inform you that no consideration will be given by this Department to the

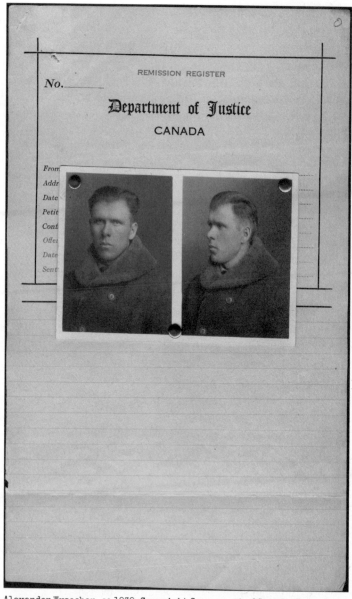

Alexander Wysochan, ca 1939. Copyright Government of Canada. Reproduced with permission of the Minister of Public Works and Government Services Canada (2011). Source: Library and Archives Canada/Department of Justice fonds/e008222388.

demand made by you for compensation in connection with the execution of your husband," wrote the deputy attorney general.

Thirty-two years later, other letters followed, from the federal director of the remission service to the Saskatchewan attorney-general's office and the RCMP.

"From time to time we have heard suggestions in this Department that Wysochan did not commit the offence for which he was hanged, and that, some years after his execution, another man made a deathbed confession of guilt," wrote the remission officer. "I should appreciate it very much if you would consult your records and let me know whether there is anything on your files to indicate that any credence should be placed on this story."

RCMP headquarters responded that a check of the file revealed nothing to suggest Wysochan was improperly convicted.

Nearly three decades had passed since his client's hanging. Still bothered by the possibility that an innocent man had died on the gallows in 1930, Prime Minister Diefenbaker made inquiries, pleading again in 1959 for another review, raising the possibility the file was incomplete—but nothing came of it.

The identity of the person who may have made the rumoured deathbed confession is never mentioned in the correspondence. During one of many political debates on the death penalty throughout the 1970s, Diefenbaker spoke of an innocent man he had defended who had gone to the gallows. Diefenbaker claimed that six months after the hanging the star prosecution witness admitted to the crime.

---

*In his memoirs, Diefenbaker refers to Stanley Kropa as the Crown's "star witness." Diefenbaker maintains he advised Wysochan to stay off the witness stand and accept a probable finding of manslaughter, which would have saved him from the noose. "I'm innocent. Why should I?" Wysochan reportedly replied.

FIRST IMPRESSIONS

Homecoming Saskatchewan 1971 was drawing people to the province from all over that summer. It was a tourism celebration filled with parades, reunions, festivals, and fairs. When an oddly dressed stranger walked into the Bank of Montreal in the town of Eastend on a Monday afternoon near the end of June, several of the customers and staff chalked it up to some sort of Homecoming publicity stunt.

The man was dressed in olive-green coveralls, had a pink towel wrapped around his waist, and wore track shoes on his feet. He was fairly imposing, perhaps six feet tall. But what actually caught most people's attention was the mask taped over his nose and upper lip. He had a ruddy complexion, at least what they could see of it around the mask. (The reddish tone was actually a layer of makeup.)

Illusions about this being some sort of ill-designed gag evaporated quickly. The armed, masked bandit interrupted a meeting between the bank manager and a customer. "I guess you know what this is?" the robber asked, as if there could be any doubt about the sawed-off shotgun in his hands. He pumped the gun and assured those inside the bank he was not joking.

He ordered staff to fill the satchel he carried with money from the tellers' tills as well as the vault. He also demanded a revolver that belonged to the bank. There were a few frantic moments while employees in the small-town bank tried to recall the location of the gun, but it too was ultimately handed over along with the bag stuffed with cash. Satisfied, the stranger ordered the six staff members and four customers—including one who had walked in on the robbery in progress—to lie flat on the floor. He then backed out the door with his withdrawal.

Outside the bank, he spied a woman sitting inside a parked car. She had been waiting for her husband, who had gone into the bank. When, instead of her husband, the stranger arrived and demanded the vehicle, she too thought it surely must be a joke. It was Homecoming, after all. The woman brushed aside what she thought must be a toy gun as she said, "You're kidding."

The response was unexpected. "I'm serious, lady," replied the man in the green coveralls and pink towel. "Get out of the car."

This time, she complied. The man slid behind the wheel of the 1970 Mercury Meteor and sped away down Redcoat Drive.

Mounties quickly moved in to set up roadblocks in the area. The remote Frenchman River Valley is a maze of rugged rolling hills, caves, buttes, and coulees. He and the thousands stolen from the bank that June 28 could be hiding almost anywhere in those badlands.

But the police narrowed down anywhere once the stolen car was found abandoned in a deep coulee near Ravenscrag, a tiny community approaching the status of a ghost town. Police officers in patrol cars and in two aircraft combed the area. Tracking dogs joined the hunt, which stretched into the next morning.

Another break came when an officer spotted the suspect at a railway crossing near Ravenscrag. But as the officer drew near, two shots rang out—aimed in the Mountie's direction. The officer responded with warning shots as the man scurried into the coulee.

Hearing the gunfire, a rancher came armed with his rifle to offer help to the Mountie. The rancher spotted the robber, as he would later tell a jury, "backing down the riverbank like a badger." Shots whizzed past the rancher, and he returned the fire until the Mounties suggested he was at risk of being caught in a crossfire and needed to leave.

As close to 20 officers surrounded the man hidden in a clump of bushes on the banks of the Frenchman River, several more shots—fired by the robber—punctuated his refusals to come out. The officers returned fire.

Finally, Richard Patrick Skelly—for that was his name—had had enough. It was a name with a blemished history. The 35-year-old was wanted in North Vancouver for armed robbery, attempted murder, and violating his parole.

The warrants described him as dangerous.

Skelly stepped from his hiding spot about a half hour before noon and sat down in the middle of a clearing to smoke a cigarette. The police officers asked the bandit to hold up his hands and give up. He shrugged, seemingly resigned to his fate.

"What's the use?" he asked.

Surrender, the officers thought with cautious optimism.

Skelly was giving up—but not in the manner the officers believed. As three Mounties carefully approached, the robber suddenly raised his gun, firing two shots at the nearest officer.

They didn't find their mark.

But an RCMP bullet did.

Near Skelly's feet lay a bag carrying roughly $26,000. More pilfered cash was stuffed in the dead man's pockets.

DOPE AND A PRAYER

Titled "Anishinabe Nation Adoption Program," the online advertisement had a list of "facts you may not know about the Indian Nations." In top spot: "Canada is not a country. Canada is a trustee with a fiduciary responsibility to the Beneficiaries, the Indian Nations and Tribes of Turtle Island."

Under "rules of Anishinabe Nation" was the notation, "No member may be permitted to exploit the land for profit. Such commercial uses of the land and or the resources shall only be permitted and or authorized by the Traditional, Inherent, Head-Chief of Anishinabe Nation."

The fee to apply for adoption was $500; $10,000 bought an adoption ceremony with an elder; and a naming ceremony with an elder also carried a $10,000 price tag. Adoption also bought protection, as a member of the "Sovereign Anishinabe Nation."

The contact on the form was Ka-Nee-Ka-Neet, whose given title was Traditional, Inherent, Grand, Continental Head-Chief of the Anishinabe Nations of Turtle Island.

It was through the website that Ka-Nee-Ka-Neet—whose full name was Kitchi O-Stew Ka-Nee-Ka-Na-Go-Shick Okimo-Wacon Ka-Nee-Ka-Neet—connected with an Ontario gardener. The middle-aged white man took the Indian name Asina Anana.

* * *

It's almost like something out of a movie. The 15-member team dressed mostly in black arrives in the dark overflow camping area at Echo Lake Provincial Park around three o'clock in the morning. Two camouflage-clad snipers with night-vision scopes leave a half hour later to take up positions closer to the two houses. A third two-man unit skulks down into the coulee beyond the houses. They are the advance sets of eyes and ears for those who will follow in the pre-dawn raid.

The advance scouts radio at 4:10 a.m.—they're all in place. Minutes later, armoured vehicles roll up the gravelled roadway leading to the two target houses. The plan calls for the nine-member assault-entry group to hit them simultaneously. They clear the first barbed-wire gate stretched across the road and are in the midst of opening a second gate when suddenly the covert operation is basking under a spotlight as if on stage. The light is coming from one of the houses.

"Lightening!" the man directing this show yells. And instantly, the RCMP's Emergency Response Team ramps up its plan of attack, quickly manoeuvring the vehicles into the ditch to get around engine blocks strewn across the roadway. A family in the first home awakes to the sound of a battering ram coming through the door, followed by the unwelcome intruders, guns drawn. At the second house, where the light came from, a man who is shouting has already stepped outside but ducks back into the house before emerging with another man.

A trail past the houses and through the trees leads to an area where a sniper hiding in the tall grass has his eyes trained on a teepee. He hears an officer shouting "Police!" on a loud-hailer.

"Fuck you. You should call me before coming on my land," someone yells in reply.

The sniper isn't the only one to hear the exchange. A head peeks out of the teepee. Within seconds, three men bolt out its door. They leave behind three hunting guns, including one that's loaded. There are eight more rifles and shotguns found in the houses.

The ensuing nine-hour chase for 15 kilometres through the Qu'Appelle Valley ends with a bang—a nine-round flash-bang. Police toss the distraction device inside a house filled with several children, where the three fugitives tried to find refuge. The men are sitting in a circle holding hands and praying they won't get shot, when the stun grenade erupts.

Asked for their names, each in turn replies: Roaming Buffalo, Flying Owl, and Asina Anana.

In all the rush, Roaming Buffalo a.k.a. Luke Andrew Zigovits, a 25-year-old visitor from Indiana, left his home movies behind in the teepee.

* * *

The camera pans a breathtakingly beautiful double rainbow brilliantly lighting up the summer evening sky over the prairie fields. As the camera moves down, it closes in for the money shot, the gold at the end of the rainbow—greenhouses filled with row upon row of lush, leafy metre-high plants.

The three hours of amateur videos are an odd blend of how-I-spent-my-summer-vacation shots coupled with a how-to tutorial. Gophers frolic, dragonflies chase mosquitoes and there is an array of sunrises, sunsets, and blue skies. But more time is dedicated to showing how the intricate "spaghetti line" of hoses waters each of the plants, the care they receive, and how they grow like weeds from knee to neck deep. In one scene, an off-camera voice yells, "Action!" and two men pull a blackout tarp over the greenery.

What the Mounties uncovered in their raid on August 21, 2005, was the largest grow-op discovered in Saskatchewan. There were 6,088 healthy marijuana plants housed mostly in the six makeshift greenhouses that each measured some seven metres by 60 metres.

If not for the officers nipping the plants before they budded out, they were a week away from full maturity, with a potential value of $7.5 million at the gram level on the street. At least, that's how the RCMP saw it.

Chief Ka-Nee-Ka-Neet a.k.a. Lawrence Hubert Age-coutay had a different vision. To the chief, as he preferred to be called, they were in the business of growing medicine, not illicit drugs. It was hemp; not pot. He was a non-Canadian, head of the sovereign Turtle Island Nation. And those gardens had the green light from him.

In testimony that was a hybrid of religion, culture, history, and the law, the chief, born Christmas Day, told jurors how the Creator had sent him the man reborn as Asina Anana, a.k.a. Chester Fernand Girard. A wise man from the east, he knew how to make things grow. The Peterborough, Ontario, man also brought 10,000 cannabis seeds and $60,000 in seed money. They called their dream the Daylight House Medicinal Industrial Research Centre for medicine and hemp products.

Two other men also came, but from the west. The brothers from British Columbia were, like Girard, drawn by a beacon of light—emanating from a computer screen with the website offering adoptions. Dodging tax collectors, they were particularly intrigued by the line that advertised tax-free status under the adoption program. They paid with goods, like material for the greenhouses, and services—sweat equity to build them. One brother authored a letter to the chief in thanks for his adoption, signing with his new name, Shung Ki Ka No Da Ko Schit Kee Uzance.

Two other young men came to help shepherd the plants to maturity. Girard's friend Zigovits, the young American he'd met in Belize, had the chief send a letter to border officials to vouch for him. And another of Girard's friends, a baby-faced 17-year-old on probation for theft in Ontario, was also able to head for greener pastures with the help of a letter from the chief that said he was coming to work at the Turtle Island cattle ranch. Both documents bore the official letterhead of the Anishinabe Nation of Turtle Island Indian Reserve and its seal, a tiny turtle in a circle.

But they didn't toil alone. About a dozen other followers, some as young as 10, pitched in with the planting, watering,

Greenhouses used for massive grow-op. Courtesy of the RCMP.

and weeding. The Mounties took care of the harvest. A five-ton farm truck hauled the cash crop to Regina, where the RCMP ensured it all went up in smoke, destroying the plants at a secret location.

The chief's defence also smouldered. It had to be rooted in the law, Justice Frank Gerein told the jury. Regardless of whether you called it hemp, medicine, or pot—marijuana plants by any other name were still illegal without a licence. And the Canadian laws applied, even on the chief's Turtle Island.

On each day of the three-week-long trial, Chester Girard, the 59-year-old de facto master gardener, wore a cream-coloured hemp suit. He often carried what was akin to his bible, a book called *The Emperor Wears No Clothes*. It is about the myriad uses for hemp and marijuana, not the similarly named children's fairy tale about a vain leader who is complimented by his loyal subjects on his new suit—even though he's wearing nothing more than a smile—after two swindlers sell him an outfit said to be invisible to those who are foolish. And who wants to admit he was a fool, after all?

The Ontario teen, who used the fake name Flying Owl, became a key witness for the Crown. "The Bri-guy"—as he was

Marijuana plants inside greenhouse at grow-op. Courtesy of the RCMP.

known in the payroll book that tracked workers' hours—said even while on the run from the teepee near the greenhouses, he still clung to the hope they really were on sovereign land, immune from Canada's drug laws. "I wasn't solidly believing it," he admitted at trial. "But I believed it could be true."

The jury accepted the two British Columbian tax dodgers were only that, and acquitted them. Zigovits pleaded guilty to drug charges long before the others fought them at trial. One of the chief's brothers was acquitted, while another, 48-year-old Robert Stanley Agecoutay, who helped with the gardens and acted as gatekeeper for unwanted people, was convicted on cultivation and possession charges, as were Girard and the chief himself, seen as the leaders of the ill-fated garden plot.

"I won't stop. I can't stop … The Creator told me to make medicine for my people," the 52-year-old unrepentant chief said before leaving court. "I forgive them," he said of the jurors.

In sentencing the men, Gerein felt the claim of hemp and medicine was all something of a smokescreen to conceal the true goal. He took note of the greenhouses hidden in a coulee behind a dense growth of trees; the two falsified documents sent by the chief to probation and border officials; a paper found at his Regina house with calculations for the expected yields, the potential profit in the millions when sold at the pound level, and a three-way split of the proceeds; the $100,000 investment in an operation that could only meet its expenses with a crop far more lucrative than hemp; invoices and receipts hidden in a ceiling at Robert Agecoutay's house that betrayed an illicit business; and the flight of Girard and the other two men in the police raid. The judge reached one conclusion: "I have absolutely no doubt that the accused were engaged in the production of a very large amount of marijuana for the express purpose of obtaining a large sum of money."

The elected band council of the Pasqua First Nation, where the unsanctioned grow-op was located, sent a letter to the court that denounced the architects of the illegal activity. "We find the actions of the individuals nothing short of reprehensible," they wrote. It called their defence "a complete and utter attack on the spiritual and cultural beliefs ... This type of testimony has not only reinforced negative stereotypes of native people but has also made a mockery of our traditions, culture, beliefs and teachings of our elders."

In a victim-impact statement, the elected chief added, "We believe drugs of all kinds weaken our bonds and are the root cause of many of our social problems. We believe it is not the Creator's way to do what these men have done."

Gerein sentenced Lawrence and Chester to six years in prison and Robert to four years.

The self-described chief of the Turtle Island Nation was back in court four years later. Provincial officials working under the Safer Communities and Neighbourhoods Act wanted him evicted after raising concerns about the frequent visitors, including known gang members and drug addicts, who came and went from his rental house in Regina. Lawrence Agecoutay challenged the jurisdiction of Canada and Saskatchewan to enact legislation affecting his rights—including the right to practise traditional medicine.

"The profile of the visitors to the rental unit is more consistent with unlawful drug activity," the hearing officer found, "than traditional religious or medicine activity."

TESTED BY FIRE

The flames dance around the floor in the room beneath the stairwell. As they curl and twist, winding around anything in their way, they gain a firmer hold. The dance grows bolder, stronger. Their reach stretches, taking the flames from the hiding place into the open hallway.

The rising smoke heralds the coming chaos.

When that spark first ignited the spilled liquid, before the swirling single flame turned to fiery pillars that reached skywards, did someone stand admiring the handiwork? Did the person marvel at the oranges and reds and blues as the intensity built? Did he pause, eagerly anticipating the arrival of the men who would have to pay grudging respect to the powerful enemy—his creation—as they battled against it?

The police thought so.

* * *

They are on relief duty, giving a break to the other teams of firefighters who have spent half of Saturday and a good part of this early Sunday morning fighting a massive blaze—and largely losing. The Federal Pioneer Electric plant lies in a $1-million ruin. Acting captain Fred Lowe and the other men are rolling up hoses when he tells his two drivers to turn the trucks around, just in case an alarm comes in and they need to get away quickly. As if on cue, the pumper truck is in the midst of backing onto Broad Street when its radio comes to life: Fire at 1140 McIntosh Street.

Pumper No. 6, carrying Lowe's crew, is the first to arrive. Flames are already shooting through the roof of a three-floor apartment when the truck pulls to a stop. Smoke pours from the windows. It is 4:30 in the morning; the 22 suites are filled with tenants who would have been asleep moments earlier. From a third-floor window near the southeast corner, one resident yells frantically for help. Two of the firefighters pull a 24-foot ladder from the pumper truck and hoist it to the window. The man, facing outward, makes it just past the midway point on the rungs when he jumps the rest of the way down. The firefighters quickly reposition to the south side of the building, moving to another window on the third floor in response to a tenant's shrieks for help.

The firefighters shout back to the man, who doesn't believe he can get out. He's told to find something to break the window, but in the cacophony of confusion, the man instead smashes it with his bare hand. He moans and suddenly disappears from the window. One of the firefighters moves up the ladder and clears away the glass with his gloved hands. The panicked, bleeding man crawls out, head first and over the shoulders of the firefighter, who catches him.

In the meantime, Lowe has taken a line of hose in through the front door. A wall of smoke and a blast of heat greet the firefighters. Shouts come at them from out of the smoke and darkness—people are still trapped on the upper floors. The brick building is becoming an oven, the heat so intense.

There is slim neutral ground in the threshold between the blistering heat inside and the freezing temperatures outside. An elderly woman, without shoes and stockings, stands inside the front door—frozen in indecision and shock between the threatening fire and the icy February darkness. She is helped into a police car for warmth.

Twice Lowe tries to get up to the second floor—only to be pushed back by the heat and smoke. On the third try, he makes it.

* * *

Melinda relished the chance of a sleepover with her grand-mother, Baba Rose. Some of her cousins were supposed to join them that night, but with other activities planned, they couldn't make the visit. The seven-year-old would have her grandma all to herself that night in suite 11. Rose Woznesensky was only recently starting to feel at home in the apartment, reshaping her life as a single working woman after burying her husband.

Upstairs in suite 19, Alexander Kostichuk, or Sandy as his friends call him, knows something of rebuilding. As a young man, he enlisted with the Saskatoon Light Infantry at the start of the Second World War and fought on the Western Front, escaping miraculously at the end of the war with only a wounded arm. The returning soldier became a travelling salesman with Hudson's Bay Wholesale in Regina. He keeps his war medals in his suite.

Not far down the hall is suite 22, the home of Gladys Evangeline Christie. She too knows about a fresh start. A gifted student, she was done high school by age 15 and earned a university degree in French, followed by her teaching degree a year later. While a teacher in small schoolhouses during the Depression, Gladys kept up her own studies, earning a masters in French. She was offered a scholarship to the Sorbonne in Paris. But her plans were waylaid by the Second World War and her mother's failing health. Gladys took a year away from teaching to nurse her mother through the woman's dying days. After her mother's death, Gladys restarted her career, joining the staff at Luther College in 1941 and finally, during a one-year sabbatical, studying at the Sorbonne.

Like most of the residents that night, they are sound asleep until the hallways fill with smoke and echo with shouts of "Fire!"

Melinda awakens to her grandmother's screams of that single word. They run out into the hallway but cannot get to the nearest staircase, at the back. Through the dark-ness and haze of acrid smoke stinging their nostrils and threatening their lungs, Rose and her granddaughter head for the front door.

Melinda gets down a couple of the stairs then collapses, overcome by the intense heat and smoke.

* * *

Battalion Chief Paul Patrick is also at the remnants of the Pioneer Electric fire when Alarm No. 139 for McIntosh Street rings out. He sees the heavy smoke and flame rolling from the windows when he arrives. It's not so unlike another apartment fire, in February one year earlier, when a blaze sparked by a careless smoker left an unprecedented nine people dead.

Patrick immediately radioes for another pumper and an ambulance as firefighters carry a man out through a window. The battalion chief enters the front door of the brick and wood building and heads down the stairs towards the basement suites. Flames fill the full width of the end of the hallway and up the back stairwell. Firefighters pour water on the blaze at the front, while another group does the same at the back of the building.

A woman holding the front door yells out that more people are trapped.

A little blonde girl sobs as she lies huddled on the stairway. Her tiny body is covered extensively by burns. Cradling the child in his arms, a firefighter carries her to an emergency vehicle.

Rose's body is not far behind, near the top of the staircase.

A police officer struggling with a face mask to help shield him from the smoke slips on the debris and water, regains his footing, and heads up the flight of stairs. He quickly hollers down for help.

Firefighter Dave Todd, not stopping to pull on a mask, rushes up the stairs. When he asks the officer where the person is, the constable points to an apartment on the right side of the second floor. Todd can't see anything in the thick black smoke so he feels around in the darkness. His hands finally land on a woman. He picks her up and carries her down the stairs, guided out by a portable light held by acting captain Ron Yanko.

Fire at Rosedale Manor, 1974. Photographer: Don Healy, courtesy of the Regina *Leader-Post*.

The fire rages for an hour, the flames reaching 20 feet above the roof, when two firefighters stumble upon another of its victims, blanketed by the heavy smoke. The body is lying prone on the landing between the second and third floors.

In the morning light, after the firefighters have taken control of the enemy, icicles hang from the shattered windows and the welcoming canopy over the front entrance marked Rosedale Manor. Rose, Gladys, and Sandy won't return.

Overcome by the smoke, 51-year-old Rose Woznesensky is dead, as is 54-year-old Alexander Kostichuk. Miss Christie, as she is called by her students, languishes in hospital with her severe burns until her death at age 60, five weeks after the fire.

In the aftermath of the fire, when there is time for reflection, several of the firefighters and tenants will recall a young man. When one firefighter was adjusting his mask before heading in to fight the flames, he handed his helmet and mitts to the young man standing near the front of the burning apartment complex.

"Anyone left in the building?" the firefighter asked.

"I don't know. I jumped out the window," the young man replied.

The young man also stood out that morning for Captain Jackson. He and his crew from Pumper No. 9 were trying to attack the fire from outside the building when he looked through a window and spotted the young man. When Jackson yelled for him to clear out, he instead turned and poked around in a closet before finally leaving. The firefighter saw him again later that morning with bandages on his burned hands. The nurse who treated him will recall that he wasn't coughing, unlike all the other tenants pulled from the smoke-filled building.

The firefighters remember how the young man after escaping the fire was fully clothed, right down to a jacket. Everyone else from the apartment block they saw that morning—really closer to the middle of the night—was wandering in their nightclothes.

As much as flames destroy, they also create—patterns and signs and evidence. When fire investigators start digging through the fire-ravaged apartment block, they trace the start of the blaze to the bottom of the stairway, in a small storage area. And, they believe, something—an accelerant—fed those flames.

Like a rash of suspicious fires in the Rosemont neighbourhood, they suspect this one is arson. Unlike the others, the consequences of this one on February 10, 1974, were devastating.

* * *

It is June 2009 when Melinda gets the phone call. Thirty-five years have passed since she was that seven-year-old, crumpled and burned on the stairs at Rosedale Manor. She has endured much since then: A year spent in a painfully tight pressure suit to flatten the scarring from burns covering 80 per cent of her body, 42 surgeries over 14 years, the stares of strangers. She defied doctors who predicted the fire would claim another life. And with the support of family and friends, Melinda carved out normalcy: School, work, dates, marriage, children. Melinda largely looked forward, not back.

But sometimes, the past would inevitably intrude, and she would find herself thinking about the fire and the person responsible for it.

"Part of me would love to know who he was," she once told the Regina *Leader-Post*, "just to have him know ... what it did to our lives."

Four years after that statement, Melinda gets the phone call from her mother. Police have charged a man with setting the fire at Rosedale Manor.

* * *

Michael John Morrison was 22 years old when he lived in suite 15 on the third floor of Rosedale Manor. He was the young man who had caught the firefighters' attention, the one who had been questioned by police the day of the fire, the prime suspect who was never charged.

He is middle-aged when a cold case detective from Regina makes a cold call, knocking on the door of Morrison's Calgary condominium more than three decades after the fire.

"I thought that was all forgotten about," says Morrison. He does not say much more. He meets the investigator's accusations with calm, cool indifference.

Morrison is a bald, frail-looking 57-year-old when he peers out from behind the glass of the prisoner's dock at Regina Provincial Court five years later, in 2009. The judge reads the charges: Manslaughter in the deaths of Rose Woznesensky, Gladys Christie, and Alexander Kostichuk; assault causing bodily harm to Melinda; and wilfully setting another fire at a seniors' complex six days before the fire at Rosedale. Morrison is not a complete stranger to a courtroom. He has outstanding charges in Calgary of trafficking in crack cocaine and of mischief for kicking out the window in a police cruiser. That arose the same night as a fire at Morrison's Calgary condominium. He won't remain a prisoner for long; the prosecution agrees to bail.

A preliminary inquiry is set for October 2010, a hearing that will test the evidence—the finding of arson; the informant who led to the charges laid 35 years after the fire; the proof that investigators have it right, beyond a reasonable doubt.

The test never comes.

Morrison is found dead that July at his new home, in Regina. He has taken his own life. But should anyone mistake it for an act of contrition, he has left a note. It is not a confession to the fire at Rosedale Manor.

The families of both those who believe in his innocence and those convinced of his guilt grieve—for those they have buried, and for the loss of any prospect for finding justice, of exonerating the wrongfully accused or proving his guilt.

Michael Morrison is remembered by his family on the first anniversary of his death. "God blesses those who hunger and thirst for justice," reads the newspaper memorial, "for they will be satisfied."

LOVER'S BLOOD

It was well past one o'clock in the morning when Frank Patrick showed up at Irene Millikin's door, his face pale and stained with smears of red.

Irene shone a flashlight up into his face.

"It is lover's blood all over me," Frank told her. "I was going to commit suicide, but it is a coward's way out."

Irene got dressed, then walked silently with Frank to his house, so he could tell his wife what he had done.

* * *

Frank Patrick knew Grace Millikin for four years, and he had loved her from the start. Grace's husband was serving overseas, and she lived with her son, Billy, in a small house outside Big River. Frank lived not far away with his wife and 11 children.

He worked sporadically and not always that hard, eking out a meagre living to support his family.

But in the spring of 1941, all he wanted to do was be with Grace. And, for a while, it seemed like she wanted to be with him, too. But one night Frank arrived at her house to find the door locked to him. He crawled in through the back window and went to Grace in her bed. She told him to leave.

"You needn't bother to come back any more," she said.

Frank left in a rage. When he got home, he confronted his wife, demanding to know whether she had visited

Grace, whether she had told Grace not to let him come around any more.

As they fought, Frank took out an axe and smashed it hard into the wooden kitchen table. He told his wife and children he would do the same to them.

Then he pulled out a box of photographs from above the stove and sat down at the table with a pair of long, sharp scissors. He looked for pictures of himself or Grace, then aimed the long scissor blades through the images, cutting off their heads in jagged circles. One was his wedding picture.

When there weren't any more, Frank gathered all the heads in his hands and put them into his wallet. Then he went upstairs for a while to think. A few minutes later, he put on a sweater and a cap and headed to Grace's house.

* * *

The fight started as soon as he walked in the door. Grace told him she'd gotten a romantic letter from another man. Frank wanted it, demanded it, but still Grace would not give it to him.

"If I don't get the letter, I get a kiss for the last time anyway," he told her.

Grace would not kiss him.

"I have given you all the kisses I am going to," she said.

A few minutes later, it was all over. Grace was lying on the floor, face down in her white polka-dotted dress.

Frank walked to see Grace's mother-in-law first. He dropped the noose he was carrying in the yard as he walked to the door. When he told Irene what he had done, she walked him home.

Frank burned his sweater, drank a cup of tea, then went back to Grace's.

He pulled down a blanket from the clothesline and lay outside his lover's house for a while, using one of her slips as a pillow. Then he hung the blanket over the window to shield her body from sight and walked towards town. He flagged down an RCMP car on the road.

"What is it, Frank?" officer J. T. Wilson asked.

"It is terrible," Frank told him.

Frank gave a full confession. He told the officer he killed her with a hammer and an axe.

"I murdered her because I loved her," he said. "Constable, you don't know what real love is."

* * *

The case went to trial four months later. Frank's wife and children were the key witnesses against him.

Frank wept as his 18-year-old daughter, Caroline, described him arriving back home on the night of Grace Millikin's murder.

"'I did it,' he was saying. 'I did it. I killed Grace,'" Caroline Patrick testified, the words filling the hushed courtroom.

"He said she was awful hard to kill, that she put up a good fight. He said he broke the hammer. If he couldn't have her, nobody else could have her."

Grace's son, Billy, also testified. The boy was so small his face barely peeked above the railing in the witness box.

"How old are you?" Justice George Taylor asked him.

"I forget," Billy answered.

Billy Millikin said he'd been sleeping, and awoke to see his mother and Frank "kind of wrestling."

"He told me to go to my grandma's," Billy said. "He said he had killed my mummy."

Billy walked out of the kitchen, never once looking down at his mother's body.

"I just looked at the door," he said.

As he walked by, he left a small footprint in his mother's blood on the house's battered wooden step.

* * *

The jury deliberated for 22 hours before declaring Frank Patrick guilty of murder. During the deliberations, jurors asked

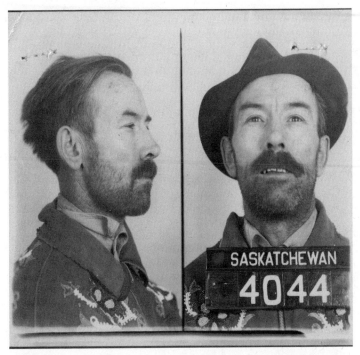

Frank Patrick. Copyright Government of Canada. Reproduced with the permission of the Minister of Public Works and Government Services Canada (2013). Source: Library and Archives Canada/Department of Justice fonds/ e10900381.

to rehear evidence given by a doctor at the Weyburn Mental Hospital, who testified Frank suffered "mental disease" and insanity, and was therefore not responsible for his actions.

While the doctor's testimony wasn't enough to keep jurors from finding Frank guilty of murder, they did make a strong recommendation for mercy.

But, despite the jury's recommendation, Justice Taylor said his hands were tied. By law, a conviction for murder could only mean the death penalty.

"I wish it were better understood by the public that in passing the sentence the judge is but the mouth piece of a provision in the statute, and required to pass the sentence whatever his own opinion may be, or whatever you might be prepared to recommend," he said.

Then he turned to Frank Patrick.

"It is my duty to impose upon you the sentence which the law requires to be imposed, and which I have no option but to impose," he said. The sentence was death.

Frank would be executed on January 16, 1942.

"Thank you," Frank said.

* * *

A week before the execution, Frank's sentence was commuted to life in prison, and he was transferred to the mental hospital in North Battleford. Frank was there for 14 years before his case was reviewed.

Justice Taylor wrote a letter against Frank's release, noting the brutality of the murder and saying he didn't even believe that Grace Millikin, "a fine looking woman of Scottish descent," had actually been involved with a man like Frank Patrick.

The judge speculated their relationship may have been "wholly illusionary" on Frank's part.

"It would appear to me inconceivable that she could have been attracted by a man of his repulsive appearance," Taylor wrote.

The judge noted Frank Patrick's IQ was measured between 76 and 78, which Taylor said was actually "rather above the average for a Slavic person."

Taylor also warned that extending leniency in the case could set a dangerous precedent for others of Slavic descent.

"We have in these Slavic immigrants in Western Canada many of his type with his low moral standards, a bullying cruel type, greatly given to drink, especially the home brews they concoct. They quarrel and fight and have little regard for consequences," the judge wrote. "Fear of punishment is the only deterrent they regard with any respect."

* * *

But Frank Patrick had other things to fear. He had terminal cancer, and though the prison doctor hadn't yet told him he was dying, Frank had been growing increasingly weak and sick.

Released from prison in October 1955, Frank went to Vancouver, where he got a little room on East Hastings Street and found work at an ink company. He earned $40 a week, until he got too sick to work.

He died in hospital on January 26, 1957. His 56th birthday. He signed his body over to the hospital.

A worker with the John Howard Society went to see Frank the week before he died. The worker said Frank had no contact with his wife or children and felt unworthy of the people who had helped him when he got out of prison. His last words were about Grace.

"On his death bed, he said she was the only woman he had ever loved," the worker wrote. "He said you don't forget those incidents, and that he had served every day of his sentence.

"He has asked for forgiveness often, and has tried to make peace with whatever god he knows."

NO STONE UNTURNED

The schoolchildren came and went, oblivious to the terrible secret trapped beneath their footsteps. She lay there as time took its toll, weeks giving way to months, then years. In the cold, damp darkness of a makeshift grave, the secret waited. For ten years, it lay buried out of reach.

Waiting.

The three young boys were determined to dig a cave that day. Playing by the ruins of the old school annex in Saskatoon, Lyle Schmidt poked around with a stick, pressing it into the packed dirt and pulling it out. When the bones turned up, Schmidt and his cousins, Dale and Terry, were excited by their discovery. A dinosaur! The boys, aged six to eight, were blissfully certain there could be nothing else in that ground. In fact, Lyle was so delighted with his treasure he took the four long bones to school the next day, April Fool's Day in 1963, for show and tell. As it turned out, his teacher wasn't all that impressed, dismissing them as dog bones and directing Lyle to wash his hands.

Lyle's mother didn't reject the matter quite so easily. While a dinosaur seemed pretty remote, she was less confident about ruling out a human being as the source. She contacted the Saskatoon Archaeological Society. When Ken Cronk checked the site where the boys had found the bones—and saw more—he knew it was time to call the police.

The remainder of a life that had been was found roughly two feet into the dirt. She—for it was the skeleton of a mature woman—had been discarded and hidden. The shallow grave was along the concrete basement wall of what had once been an annex providing extra classrooms for Bedford Road Collegiate. The building at Avenue F and 21st Street had housed the city's Hebrew School until the school board bought it in 1957 to provide space for the burgeoning high school population. No longer needed, the aging annex had been demolished.

The woman buried there lay on her right side, the ground beneath her cradling the wounds that would reveal how she had met death. It had no doubt come painfully and in full fury. Bones on her right side had been mangled and crushed, the result of a brutal beating. "An instrument may have been used," a doctor would later tell the inquest.

There were small hints of a life, and a death—remnants of a green coat wrapped around her head and women's stockings that held the bones of her legs. A tiny, discoloured ring circled the finger of a hand that had perhaps tried, in futile desperation, to ward off the deadly blows.

Who was she? And who had ended her life? It was as big a mystery as the brutal and unsolved murder almost a year earlier of nurse Alexandra Wiwcharuk, the 23-year-old beauty queen whose battered body had been left under a mound of dirt by the river, her hand reaching out from the impromptu grave.

In the spring of 1963, Saskatoon police knew of two women who had been reported missing and never found. No one had seen Kathleen Grace Johnston since October 20, 1953. That's the day the 26-year-old brunette, dressed in a green pinstriped suit with red shoes and a matching handbag, got off a trolley bus downtown as she headed to work at the Gem Café.

Jessie Christina Randall had also disappeared in 1953. It was sometime in August when anyone last remembered seeing the 53-year-old Saskatoon woman, who lived a few blocks from the school. Her dentist was among the last people to see her before she had vanished. Jessie was supposed to have picked up a set of false teeth around the time of her disappearance. She never did.

Photographs and dental impressions of Randall were compared with the skeleton, which had no teeth, nor had any been found in the grave. The experts were certain they had found Jessie Randall.

In the summer of 1953, she had taken a job doing kitchen work at banquets, teas, and special events hosted by the Saskatoon Hebrew School, like its annual harvest festival. Each fall, a Succoth—a sort of shed with a slatted roof from which grains could be hung, leaving the sky visible between the slats—was erected in front of the north entrance of the school, as it was back then. The structure usually remained in place for seven days, then it was taken down by the caretaker. When the succoth was placed in its usual spot, it would have covered Jessie's grave.

Leonard Stevens was 70 years old when he took the witness stand at the inquest into Jessie's death in June 1963. Almost a decade had passed since Leonard had last seen Jessie. But he was very certain of what he did and did not know.

Leonard had been the caretaker at the school from 1951 to August 1953. He had hired Jessie to help with the dishwashing, except he knew her as Irene or Betty. He was sure the last time she had worked for him was on August 7, 1953. She had helped him prepare for a banquet, and when she left that night, it was with a man, he said. Leonard knew nothing about how she died or how she came to be buried by the school.

"No," he said repeatedly when questioned at the inquest by lawyer T. D. R. Caldwell about whether or not Jessie had died in his presence, or if he had killed her. "I had nothing to do with it," Leonard insisted.

Leonard was a collector, a bit of a pack rat really. So it wasn't so surprising when police opened a suitcase that belonged to Leonard and found it stuffed with what, at first blush anyway, looked like what one officer would call "an awful lot of trash." There were letters, old receipts, penny matches, stubs of pencils, pieces of army clothing, ties, jackknives, keys, perfume, shaving lotion, and three sets of eyeglasses. He couldn't really remember where most of it had come from, but Leonard was quite certain that none of it came from Jessie, who had worn glasses. He had bought a three-dollar box of things at an auction sale, he said. He took the box home, dumped the contents into the black suitcase, and forgot about them.

A tube of lipstick and a lady's brooch lay among the items in the suitcase.

The brooch was missing a rhinestone just like the one found with Jessie's body.

Jessie Randall's killing remains unsolved. Kathleen Grace Johnston is still missing.

DAY OF THE DEAD

Fourteen people gather in a semicircle around the grave. Their silence is broken by the steady wind ushering in the approaching fall, and the solitary voice of the minister trying to be heard above it. Heads bowed and hands clasped reverently in front of them or behind their backs, the men and women have come to pay their last respects to someone they never met, never knew, and never heard called by name. They know something of his death, but virtually nothing of his life.

He was a smoker and a reader; he travelled alone; and he had reached a point in his journey when there seemed to be nowhere else to go—that little they do know. But if he enjoyed the cigarettes or the novel he carried, if he preferred solitude or felt lonely, and why he gave up—all of those things are left to the imagination.

"We don't know what stresses and tragedies had affected his life," says Reverend Canon Patrick Tomalin. As he leads the service, offering prayers and Bible readings for the deceased and those touched by his death, the minister stands beside a grey, granite, rectangular headstone. It is engraved with a Biblical inscription, the date of death, and a name.

It is not the name of the man who was buried here five months ago.

"We come because we care about a stranger who seemed to have no one to care for him," Tomalin says during the memorial service. "May this be a comfort to this man's family," he adds, "if they ever learn what happened to him."

What happened was tragic; but what happened afterwards—in the months, years, and more than a decade that passed—compounded the loss. Because nothing happened. No family or distant relative or friend—no one—came looking for the young man buried in the Regina graveyard. No one missed him. No one ever put a name to the unidentified man.

The words on the top of the headstone read: Died in a railroad incident July 28, 1995; Come to me all you who are weary and burdened Matt. 11:28.

* * *

It is closing in on 3:30 in the afternoon when the freight train approaches Regina from the west. Four locomotives pull 104 loaded grain cars, bearing down on the city at almost 70 kilometres an hour.

The engineer leans on the whistle as the train nears Thirteenth Avenue and Courtney Street, on the city's outskirts. A man, walking alongside the CP Rail mainline, has been waiting. He briefly heads away from the track to drop his knapsack out of the way, but then very deliberately walks back to the rails. Approaching from the south, he places his head down on the track. He has mere seconds to wait, to reconsider perhaps.

The horrified engineer throws on the brakes, trying in vain to bring nearly 14,500 tons of steel and cargo to an abrupt stop.

When police come to investigate the death, officers find a blue canvas knapsack, a body, and absolutely nothing that reveals who this man is or why he chose to die here on this day.

In the absence of a name, features become his identity: Caucasian, blue eyes, in his mid-20s to early 30s, about five foot nine, 140 to 160 pounds, circumcised, sparse chest hair. He is clean-shaven and the coarse, medium-brown hair on his head is groomed and worn short, just above the collar at the back. He kept the nails on his long, thin fingers trimmed, and his toenails clipped short. He doesn't have any moles or birthmarks of any note, and no tattoos.

He wore faded Essentials brand blue jeans, white socks, size 12 ½ blue-and-white Reebok high-top running shoes on his size 9 ¾ feet, and a light grey T-shirt emblazoned with red letters outlined in blue that read "Boca Authentic" on the front. Over that was a black denim collared shirt, a size medium Rough and Tough Chams brand, with buttons. A yellow-gold embroidered emblem—a crown atop a circle with a capital letter *C* at the centre and two branches of leaves crossed at the bottom—adorns the left pocket. Another T-shirt he carried is marked with Padova City Resorts Inc., lakeside property near Kamloops, British Columbia. The brands and logos may mean something, perhaps a clue to where this man lived or worked or even shopped—or absolutely nothing, like so many of the seemingly promising leads.

For more than a decade, much of what police officers thought they knew about the dead man came from a hitchhiker. He remembered the young man well; they had travelled together for several days. He recalled how his new friend seemed inexperienced in the life of a drifter, how he was well-mannered and used a knife and fork to eat his hamburger, how he talked about a girlfriend named Kathy, how he seemed to know a lot about the ocean and referred to "back east," and how he called himself Dave.

Only problem is, none of it is true. The man with no identity was a victim of mistaken identity. The hitchhiker was confused about his fellow traveller; it was never the suicidal young man.

Over the years, the dead man's image, created by an artist using autopsy photos, is circulated locally, nationally, and internationally. And still he does not have a name. DNA tests, fingerprints, and dental records that show two root canals on his upper front teeth yield nothing.

What is known? He left this world with little in his possession. The pockets of his jeans carried a comb, $45.05, and a small, silver brooch in the shape of a stemmed rose.

Maybe the keepsake meant something to him, or perhaps it was nothing more than a trinket discovered on a street somewhere.

Artist's sketch of John Doe and his rose keepsake. Source: Regina Police Service.

His knapsack held a yellow T-shirt and a blue one, an open pack of du Maurier cigarettes, a green Bic lighter, a pen bearing a logo for C. U. and C. Health Services Society in Vancouver, British Columbia, and a novel titled *Under the Volcano*. Penned by English author Malcolm Lowry, who once lived near Vancouver, the partly autobiographical tragedy tells the story of an alcoholic consul in Mexico, of failures, and of death. The backdrop is Mexico's Day of the Dead.

It is a holiday set aside to remember and pray for loved ones who have died—kind of like the 14 people who gathered

John Doe's grave in Regina, 2011. Photographer: Troy Fleece, courtesy Regina *Leader-Post*.

that September day in 1996 for the stranger. It was actually the second service held for him. At the first, when the unnamed and unclaimed body was interred in an unmarked grave almost nine months after his death, only the coroner attended.

That didn't seem right to one woman. Anonymously, she launched a small campaign to raise money so the grave could be marked. Within three days, 11 people had given $390. When Remco Memorials donated the headstone and a flower vase, the money collected went instead to assist a suicide prevention line and to pay for perpetual care of the grave. The vase is often filled with artificial flowers.

The woman was among those at his grave for the memorial, prompted by her efforts. "He had no one," she explained to a reporter. "He was away from home."

For the 10th anniversary of the man's death, the anonymous benefactor agreed to be named as the Saskatchewan Coroner's Office drew attention to the tragedy in hopes of trying once again to identify the dead man.

"I just felt so sorry for him, that's all," she told a reporter.

Her name is Barbara Beck.

His name is unknown, but the face of his headstone reads John Doe.

TRICK PLAY

The game was a nailbiter. With a six-game winning streak at home on Regina's Taylor Field, a win against the visiting Argonauts seemed guaranteed for the Riders. That was, until the disastrous fourth quarter. A couple of fake plays by Toronto's special teams stole the anticipated victory. Afterwards, in explaining the 24-19 loss for reporters, linebacker Mike McCullough summed it up simply: "We let our guard down."

Rob watched the game with friends and family at his uncle's house in Bladworth that Saturday, October 9, in the fall of 2010. When it was over, he met up with a co-worker from the chemical plant where Rob was a supervisor. They left the local bar around midnight and headed out in Rob's Chevy Cobalt for the home of a young woman in nearby Davidson. Having recently made the last payment, he was so proud of that car.

* * *

It's around 2:30 the next afternoon when Constable Alan Cassidy clocks the black two-door doing upwards of 143 kilometres per hour on Circle Drive in Saskatoon. The driver, who admits he doesn't have a licence, begs the officer not to seize the car. Polite and co-operative, the young man accepts his two traffic tickets and convinces Cassidy to let him leave the car parked at the side of the road. A downed computer system doesn't allow the officer to check if the Cobalt should be impounded. The driver chats about farming as the constable gives him a ride to Confederation Mall.

Roberto Joseph Vicente, the 25-year-old from Bladworth, and his beloved vehicle, have yet to be reported missing.

Telling them he bought the car, Darak More, the ticketed driver, has friends give him a ride back to the vehicle parked on the roadside. He waits until almost midnight, then drives to Davidson, meeting with Devin Schmit. The two men strip the Cobalt of its stereo and speakers and leave the car in an old garage at an abandoned farmyard west of town. They empty two, five-litre jugs of diesel on the car and shed, and set them ablaze. Some people see the smoke, but it isn't until the late afternoon of the next day, Wednesday, October 13, that the source is discovered. Scarred and damaged, the smouldering black 2006 Chevy Cobalt is nearly unrecognizable.

Rob's mother had reported her son missing one day earlier.

It wasn't like him to miss his brother's birthday or the Thanksgiving family gathering that weekend. He wouldn't ordinarily ignore the frantic phone calls and texts made to his phone. Rob and his uncle usually travelled to work together, and when Rob didn't pick him up, the family knew for certain something wasn't right.

Family, friends, neighbours, police, and even strangers join in the search for Roberto Vicente. With dread and hope, they scour sloughs, gullies, farms, sheds, and abandoned buildings—the sheer possibilities overwhelming. His mother Pam lies awake at night, fretting for her eldest son as the days grow colder. The search moves from fall to winter, leaving a family in agonizing limbo, mulling over scenarios: Hurt? Lost? Held? Tortured? Amnesic?

Meanwhile, Darak More installs his new stereo and speakers in his bedroom at a home in Davidson where he's staying and shows them off to visitors—at least, until the RCMP seize them a little more than a week after Rob vanishes. By the door, the officer spies a plastic bag containing some of More's belongings. Inside is a copy of the *StarPhoenix* news-paper; the front-cover story is titled "Where's Rob Vicente?"

Rob Vicente's burned-out car. Courtesy of the RCMP.

* * *

At a party in early December, More sits smoking a cigarette in a truck with a couple of other men. A drunken More asks if they've heard about a guy missing from Davidson. He and his buddy wanted the guy's stereo, he tells them, and when that guy wouldn't give it up, they shot him and buried the body. As More talks on a cellphone in the cab of the truck, the two men also overhear his conversation about a drug deal. More threatens his drug connection that if he won't sell him some dope, he'll disappear. Just like Rob.

Devin Schmit is talking too, telling an acquaintance in late December and early January how he was involved in a murder and buried a body. He's worried the Mounties, who have brought in a cadaver dog from Calgary, just might stumble upon it. But the dog's ability is foiled by the cold temperatures and snow in the dead of winter.

More and Schmit are still talking when the Mounties arrest them in February 2011. After his confession to police, Schmit phones his mother. "I shot him. It happened so fast," he tells her. "It happened so fast, before I even knew what I was doing, it was done. Now you see why I was so scared." And, he adds, "Twenty-five years is a long time."

On Valentine's Day, it's More who takes officers to Rob's body, buried not far from where he was shot four months earlier, an empty bottle of muriatic acid nearby.

When Schmit was asked to take officers there, he replied, "What's in it for me?"

* * *

Nearly two years pass before Rob Vicente's mother, Pam, gets the opportunity to confront her son's killers, to try to make them appreciate all that they took so callously, so lightly. Dressed in black with a yellow ribbon on her lapel, she pays tribute to her firstborn, recalling a little boy's arms wrapped around his mother's neck, his sweet cheek pressed next to hers—and how she wasn't there to comfort and hold him when he died a young man. "Rob died alone," Pam Vicente tells her son's killers as her tears give way. Needing to see what was once her son, Pam explains to them how she was allowed into a room where he lay in a body bag, a sheet draped overtop. "That was where I said goodbye to my once handsome, once full-of-life son."

As Darak Andrew More and Devin Riel Joseph Schmit—close in age to their victim at 21 and 23—plead guilty to second-degree murder, Rob's family and many others in the packed courtroom wonder about a world in which a car stereo carries more value than a human life.

"Chilling," prosecutor Bill Jennings later says.

At the gathering in Davidson, Rob had agreed to use his Chevy for a beer run to Bladworth. They stopped on the way back at the Shell service station in Davidson. Rob, who wasn't in any shape to drive, remained in the back seat with the young woman hosting the gathering. Schmit stayed behind at her home to mind her children.

Meanwhile, Darak More, who was driving, got an eyeful and earful of Rob's car stereo system—an Alpine with a touch screen CD player and Kicker subwoofers. "Turn it up, turn it up," Rob said, reaching over from the back seat to show off the stereo to friends at the Shell. "Let him hear my subs."

An hour after the first trip, More was back in the driver's seat after asking Rob if they could run to Davidson for cigarettes. When More returned to the party two hours later, shortly before 6 a.m., he came alone—telling all but one of his friends that Rob had ditched him at the service station and driven off. To Schmit, he confided the truth—they had driven around in the Cobalt until Rob passed out. Then More parked the car and its sleeping owner in a farmyard and came back. He and Schmit returned to the farmyard, owned by Schmit's family, on the outskirts of Davidson.

They would steal more than the stereo.

Schmit grabbed a .22-calibre rifle and some bullets from the shop and returned to the parked car. The two men discussed how, if they fired it too close to the house, someone might hear. To reduce the risk, More drove the car to the furthest treeline in the shelterbelt and parked. Schmit sat in the back with the gun while Rob, leaning against the door, slept in the front passenger seat. When More pulled the door open, Rob's upper body slid to the ground. That's when Schmit fired at the back of the young man's head.

More would later tell police he heard Rob say, "Darak, help me." Schmit pulled the trigger a second time, hitting Rob behind the right ear.

After dragging Rob's body deeper into the row of trees, Schmit fired once more into the middle of Rob's back to "finish him off." They stripped Rob of his jeans, green T-shirt, and black sweater before covering his body with tree branches.

And they walked away, going home to sleep.

They returned later to bury him in a shallow grave. More drove off with Rob's Chevy Cobalt and the coveted stereo and headed for Saskatoon.

* * *

Darak Andrew More, 2012. Photographer: Michael Bell, courtesy Regina *Leader-Post*.

As the two confessed killers sat slumped on the hard wooden bench of the prisoner's box, they had little choice but to hear how that incomprehensible act had reverberated, irrevocably changing lives.

There were a record 25 victim impact statements—one for every year of Rob Vicente's life. They came from his mother, father, two brothers, aunts, uncles, cousins, friends, townsfolk, and the mayor of Davidson.

They remembered Rob's sense of humour, love of music, engaging personality, goofy moves on the dance floor, heartwarming laugh, and beautiful smile. They described him as a kind and gentle soul. And they mourned what would never be: Marriage, children, old age.

"Rob was 25 years old," Pam Vicente stood and told his killers. "That was not enough time, 25, too short years. How can 25 years equal life?"

For Rob's brother Daniel, who marked his 24th birthday the day Rob disappeared, every missed phone call or text

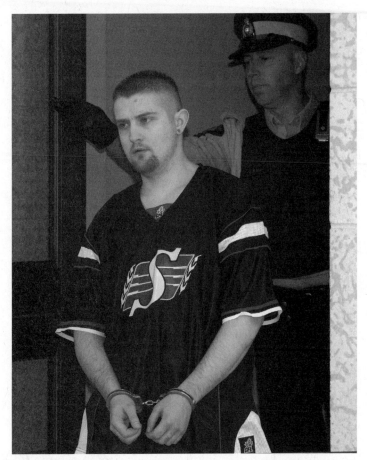

Devin Riel Joseph Schmit, 2012. Photographer: Michael Bell, courtesy Regina *Leader-Post*.

without a response afterwards brought back the horror of the days when he had tried frantically to reach his brother.

Their father, Fernando, remembered the pride Rob took in his new stereo, constantly adjusting to get it right, the boom still echoing in his father's ears long after. "My son's life for a stereo," he wrote in his statement. "How can anyone have such little regard for someone's life?"

One statement was noticeably absent. Robbie, as she called him, was a favourite of his grandmother's. He had been chosen by the elderly woman to carry her urn at her funeral someday. Instead, she sat wracked by sobs at her grandson's funeral, and never really recovered. Almost all of the family's victim impact statements spoke of how Rob's death seemed to hasten hers. She awoke in the night in May 2011 and called out for her Robbie.

She passed away two days later on what would have been his 26th birthday.

All of Rob Vicente's family spoke of the night he was "taken." But More and Schmit had also stolen something else in a small town where, as one resident wrote, "everybody knows everybody and watches out for everyone."

"We now know that evil is not exclusive to large cities, and it exists in our small, safe communities," wrote Corey Eddie. "We are forever changed."

Rob Vicente was like countless others who began their Thanksgiving weekend watching a Riders game.

Rob never saw More and Schmit coming, never anticipated the trick play.

In the prisoner's dock in October 2012 as one after another of those victim impact statements was read, Devin Schmit wore a black Riders jersey. That coming weekend, on Thanksgiving, the Saskatchewan Roughriders would play the Toronto Argonauts.

Schmit also wore black on his cheek. Between the time of his arrest and his guilty plea, Schmit had added a jailhouse tattoo. Etched in ink was a tiny teardrop beneath his left eye—the mark of a killer.

"This kind of thing happens to other families," Rob Vicente's uncle wrote to the court. "You never think it will happen to yours."

SOURCES AND REFERENCES

THE KEY—Court transcript and documents; *Regina Leader-Post*; interviews.

BITTER WIND—Library and Archives Canada file.

WHEELS OF JUSTICE—Court transcript; Library and Archives Canada file; *Regina Leader-Post*; *Winnipeg Free Press*.

A ROSE BY ANY OTHER NAME—Court transcripts and documents; *Regina Leader-Post*; *Saskatoon StarPhoenix*; *Edmonton Journal*; Canadian Press; *Winnipeg Free Press*.

INSIDE MAN—*Regina Morning Leader*; Saskatchewan Archives Board's court files R v Eddie Norris, R v Hart Henshaw, Leroy Compton, Axel Pierson, Jack R. Howard (a.k.a. J. B. Shelton); Website http://gent-family.com/Bienfait/leedellagebio.html.

AN UNCOMMON CRIMINAL—*Regina Morning Leader*; Saskatchewan Archives Board's court documents.

HOODWINKED—Saskatchewan Archives Board's Department of the Attorney General files; *Regina Morning Leader*; *Saskatoon Star-Phoenix*; *Regina Leader-Post*.

PRAIRIE CHICKENS—Court transcript; Library and Archives Canada file; *The Daily Phoenix*.

OF MEN AND MADNESS—Court transcript; Library and Archives Canada file; *Regina Daily Leader*; *Moose Jaw Murders and Other Deaths* by Bruce D. Fairman, Home Town Press, 2003.

FREE RANGE—Regina RCMP historical case unit; trial transcript and court documents; "Local nutritionist publishes own book" by Ron Walter, *Moose Jaw Times-Herald Community Sun*, Sept. 11, 2005, p. 4; *Moose Jaw Times-Herald*; Saskatchewan Association of Chiefs of Police missing persons Website (http://www.sacp.ca/).

THE SCISSORS GRINDER—Library and Archives Canada file.

THE IDEA MAN—Saskatchewan Court of Appeal file; *Saskatoon StarPhoneix*; *Ottawa Citizen*; Canadian Press; *Toronto Star*; *Montreal Gazette*; *Kingston Whig-Standard*; *Globe and Mail*; *Windsor Star*; *Kitchener-Waterloo Record*; "The death penalty; for the thinking man is a godsend," from Maltby's interview with the *London Free Press* as quoted in the *Ottawa Citizen* November 19, 1993, page B6.

A DIFFERENT CAT—Regina RCMP historical case unit; *Regina Leader-Post*; court documents; unidentified magazine article.

OLD BLUE EYES—*Regina Leader-Post*; *Gainesville Sun*; reporter's notes; interview.

WRONG TURN—Regina RCMP historical case unit; *Regina Leader-Post*; *Winnipeg Free Press*.

FANCY WORK—*Moose Jaw Evening Times*; Library and Archives Canada file, RCMP fonds; *Moose Jaw Murders and Other Deaths* by Bruce D. Fairman, Home Town Press, 2003.

THE SMOKING GUNMAN—*Regina Morning Leader*; *Regina Leader Post*; *Saskatoon Phoenix*; *Saskatoon StarPhoenix*; *Glasgow Herald*; *London Times*; *Mahoney's Minute Men* by Chris Stewart and Lynn Hudson, Modern Press, 1978.

THE INTERVIEW—Court transcripts and documents; *Saskatoon StarPhoenix*.

DAIRY GLASS—Court transcript; Library and Archives Canada file; *Prince Albert Herald*; *Saskatoon StarPhoenix*.

BEHIND THE EIGHT BALL—Court documents; Regina Integrated Drug Unit; reporter's notes; interviews.
NO FIXED ADDRESS—National Parole Board report; interviews; decision of the Alberta Court of Appeal; decision of the Federal Court of Appeal; *Regina Leader-Post*; *Calgary Herald*; *Edmonton Journal*; Canadian Press; *Vancouver Sun*.

ONE OF THE BEST KILLING ROOMS—*Saskatoon StarPhoenix*; Saskatchewan Archives Board's Department of the Attorney General files; *The Memory Box: 100 years of Policing in Saskatoon* by Susan Grant, Saskatoon Police Service, 2003; City of Saskatoon Website (www.saskatoon.ca).

DETERMINATION—Reporter's notes; court documents; National Parole Board report.

LOVERS' WHISPERS—Library and Archives Canada file, including letters, documents and transcripts; *Regina Leader-Post*.

THE CHASE—*Regina Leader-Post*; Regina Police Service.

HALF-BAKED—*Regina Leader-Post*; *Saskatoon StarPhoenix*.

HUSH—Regina RCMP historical case unit; *Regina Leader-Post*; *Swift Current Sun*.

$320—Library and Archives Canada file.

DEVIL'S TOOLS—Parole Board of Canada reports; reporters' notes; *Regina Leader-Post*; *Globe and Mail*; Regina Correctional Centre Escape Report.

THE LAST STRAW—Court transcript; Library and Archives Canada files; *Saskatoon StarPhoenix*.

A BUDDING CAREER—Court documents; *Saskatoon StarPhoenix*; *Ontario Business Magazine*; *Edmonton Journal*; *Sudbury Star*.

SUSPICION—Saskatchewan Archives Board's Department of the Attorney General files.

BOILING POINT—Court transcript; Library and Archives Canada file; *One Canada—Memoirs of the Right Honourable John G. Diefenbaker: The Crusading Years 1895-1956* by John G. Diefenbaker, Macmillan of Canada, Toronto, 1975; *Saskatoon StarPhoenix*; *Manitoba Free Press*; *Morning Leader*.

FIRST IMPRESSIONS—*Regina Leader-Post*; *Saskatoon StarPhoenix*; *Maple Creek News*; *Swift Current Sun*.

DOPE AND A PRAYER—Court documents; reporter's notes; *Regina Leader-Post*; Website www.anishinabe.org.

TESTED BY FIRE—*Regina Leader-Post*; reporter's notes; interviews; *Langley Advance*; Regina Police Service Website (www.reginapolice.ca); Regina Fire Department; *Globe and Mail*; *Calgary Sun*; *Calgary Herald*.

LOVER'S BLOOD—Library and Archives Canada file; *Prince Albert Daily Herald*.

NO STONE UNTURNED—*Saskatoon StarPhoenix*; Saskatoon Police Service; *The Memory Box: 100 years of Policing in Saskatoon* by Susan Grant, Saskatoon Police Service, 2003.

DAY OF THE DEAD—*Regina Leader-Post*; Coroner's Office; Regina Police Service; *Calgary Herald*.

TRICK PLAY—Reporter's notes; interviews; *Regina Leader-Post*; *Saskatoon StarPhoenix*.

ABOUT THE AUTHOR

Born and raised in Regina, Barb Pacholik is a graduate of the University of Regina's School of Journalism. Since 1988 she has worked as a reporter at the Regina *Leader-Post*, where she has spent most of her career covering crime and justice issues.

Her first two books—*Sour Milk and Other Saskatchewan Crime Stories*, and *Paper Cows and More Saskatchewan Crime Stories*—were co-authored with colleague Jana G. Pruden. This is Barb's third collection of true Saskatchewan crime stories.

Also in this series:

Sour Milk & Other Saskatchewan Crime Stories

Paper Cows & More Saskatchewan Crime Stories

visit us on-line: UOFRPRESS.CA